# PRAISE FOR *THE LAST LETTER*

"If you feel frazzled, depressed, angry or even longing for something that you can't really define, then this is the book you want to read. Joy, connection and peace—hallmarks of your most authentic life—are all waiting for you. It begins with a willingness to be vulnerable, and in this book, Andy shows you the way in."

### —LAURA BAKOSH, PH.D., Co-Founder Inner Explorer, Inc.

"I find few books that touch me in a way that endures. This is one of those rare exceptions. A narrative of pathos and wisdom, a personal, intimate account with deep insight and inspiration for anyone looking to understand life's compelling contradictions and grace, generously and courageously shared with the world. As a dedication to our common friend, Cees de Bruin, to whom Andy Chaleff was closest, nothing could be more fitting or beautiful."

### —PETER KOENIG, Founder of The Money Work and The Money Seminar

"I was hooked from page one. A beautiful and moving portrayal with heart, vulnerability and soul throughout."

### —LARA TABATZNIK, Co-Founder 42 Acres

"I couldn't put it down. Andy's unvarnished storytelling is inspiring. You will live life differently after finishing this book."

### —JEFF MCCLELLAN, Founding Director of the first MC2 STEM High School and Sta

"We walk through life sometimes thinking we are really being transparent with our love. Andy wakes us up to the realization that we haven't even started. Don't let a minute go by. Pick up this book."

—**JOANN LOVASCIO**, Teacher / Therapist / Core Energetics Practitioner

"Spending time with Andy has been transformational for me. Reading this book is the next best thing."

—**JOSH WHITON**, Founder of TransLoc and MakeSoil

"You may not even know what you've learned, but your life will be more authentic, connected, and downright thrilling."

—**JEFF LIEBERMAN**, Host of Discovery Channel's *Time Warp*

"You are invited to the freedom and joy of living in honesty, gratitude, and awe. This work guides people back to true north."

—**TIM SHRIVER**, Former CEO Jesuit Volunteer Corps

"Andy has taught me the power of vulnerability. I am truly indebted to him."

—**KELLEY MCCABE**, Founder of eMindful

"Andy shares valuable life lessons learned along his path from debilitating trauma to self discovery. An incredible story."

—**GINO YU**, Associate Professor Hong Kong Polytechnic University

"Nothing has helped me understand, process, and heal my emotions more than this book. I used to fight and repress my emotions because I was afraid of them. Andy has taught me how to embrace them and use them to guide me to a life of action and meaning."

**—STEPHEN PALMER**, Author of *Manifest Destiny*

"There are authors who repeat worn-out dogma from other thinkers, and those who speak with the authority that can only come from direct experience. Andy Chaleff is obviously the latter, and the inner work he has done on his own emotions is both instructional and inspirational. I highly recommend this book for anyone who wants to learn how to trust themselves to find their own answers to life's deepest questions."

**—MICHAEL BUNTING**, Bestselling Author of *The Mindful Leader*

"*The Last Letter* is an extraordinary book by an extraordinary human being. Written with rare candor and insight, Andy shares his remarkable life and gives the reader a front row seat to encounter the archetypal hero's journey. In taking your seat and enjoying the book, I trust that there will be gifts received and truths accessed that are applicable to all of our lives. This was my experience—beyond the book being an intriguing and immensely enjoyable read, I benefited from much wisdom. I hope you do so as well. If you also take the opportunity to write your Last Letter, it may just change your life."

**—WILL PYE**, Author of *Blessed with a Brain Tumor*

*The Last Letter*

by *Andy Chaleff*

Published by

**◄ köehlerbooks** ™

210 60th Street
Virginia Beach, VA 23451
212-574-7939
www.koehlerbooks.com

# THE
# LAST
# LETTER

## EMBRACING PAIN TO
## CREATE A MEANINGFUL LIFE

# ANDY CHALEFF

VIRGINIA BEACH
CAPE CHARLES

# TABLE OF CONTENTS

**WELCOME . . . I**

Pain is not a malicious enemy to be conquered, but rather a loving friend to surrender to.

**CHAPTER I: THE DAY I DIED . . . 6**

I lose what I cherish most—my mother. I feel completely alone in the world and life loses all meaning.

**CHAPTER 2: DROWNING IN THE PAIN . . . 9**

I go from an outgoing, fun-loving person to a hermit. I'm completely detached from life.

**CHAPTER 3: THE RAGING MONSTER AND THE LOVING SAINT . . . 14**

My father, who suffered from bipolar disorder, had severe emotional swings. My mother was my anchor and comfort in life.

**CHAPTER 4: MY LAST LETTER . . . 19**

While in college, I write a letter of love and appreciation to my mother. It's the last thing she will ever read from me.

**CHAPTER 5: A HOPE FOR PEACE . . . 23**

I experience a moment of feeling protected, safe, loved, cradled in support. I get a glimpse of the possibility of inner peace.

**CHAPTER 6: EXPANDING MY INNER AND OUTER HORIZONS . . . 28**

I realize I have nothing left to lose—I can become anyone I want to become. I start exploring everything from a blank-slate perspective.

**CHAPTER 7: VENTURING INTO THE OUTBACK . . . 34**

Dropping my social scripts, I decide to set off on an adventure to Australia.

**CHAPTER 8: LEARNING TO LET GO . . . 39**

I see the addiction in pain. If we tell ourselves the same story long enough, we become addicted to its outcome.

**CHAPTER 9: LIFE AND DEATH ON A RANCH . . . 43**

I take a job on a remote ranch in the outback and experience the harsh realities of life.

**CHAPTER 10: GOING WALKABOUT . . . 49**

I decide to take a year off from school and travel the world.

**CHAPTER 11: EXPLORING CHINA . . . 57**

My travels take me to China, where everything is different. Yet at the same time, I see the similarities in our universal humanity.

**CHAPTER 12: LEARNING TO QUESTION MY THOUGHTS . . . 73**

I return home and resume college. I find a mentor who helps me understand the difference between mere opinions and true thinking.

**CHAPTER 13: A CLASH AND A CONNECTION . . . 79**

I move to Japan for a work abroad program. I'm shocked by cultural differences, and make a dear friend.

**CHAPTER 14: CONFUSED BY COMMUNAL RESPONSIBILITY . . . 85**

The conformity I witness in Japan is tied to a deep sense of responsibility to the group, which is a shock to my American perspective.

**CHAPTER 15: STUDYING RELIGION-AND MYSELF . . . 89**

I study Japanese religion, and in the process learn more about myself.

**CHAPTER 16: IRRECONCILABLE DIFFERENCES . . . 95**

As much as I appreciate Japanese culture, the differences are too much for me.

**CHAPTER 17: EXPERIENCING "ISHIN-DENSHIN" . . . 99**

Japan teaches me that deep human connection, which transcends words, is the most beautiful and healing thing in the world.

**CHAPTER 18: AN UPWARD AND INWARD TREK . . . 103**

After circling the Annapurna mountain range in Nepal, I come off the mountain a different man.

**CHAPTER 19: DISINHERITED . . . 108**

After returning home, my father disinherits me for not following his preferred career path for me.

**CHAPTER 20: SWISS COLD, TO VIENNESE OPPORTUNITY . . . 113**

I move to Switzerland with my girlfriend. I struggle integrating into the culture, so we pursue a job opportunity.

**CHAPTER 21: RISING HIGH AND FEELING LOW . . . 118**

I take a job as a marketing director and begin to lose touch with the curiosity that made my life so beautiful. I replace it with money and status, which makes me feel empty.

**CHAPTER 22: A HOLE IN MY SOUL . . . 123**

I break up with my girlfriend and fill my schedule with distractions to escape my inner emptiness.

**CHAPTER 23: SEEING THE TRUTH FOR THE FIRST TIME . . . 129**

I meet a mentor, Cees, who shows me things about myself that I've never seen before.

**CHAPTER 24: WHO ARE YOU? . . . 135**

    With Cees's help, I begin seeing that I am not my thoughts, beliefs, or opinions. There is something deeper.

**CHAPTER 25: FROM CORPORATE DIRECTOR TO UNEMPLOYED STUDENT . . . 140**

    I quit my job, sell all my possessions, and move into a tiny attic in Amsterdam to be mentored by Cees.

**CHAPTER 26: EMBRACING MY EMOTIONS WITHOUT RESISTANCE . . . 146**

    I learn that judging emotions as "good" or "bad" greatly inhibits my ability to embrace life in all its fullness and richness.

**CHAPTER 27: BEYOND RIGHT AND WRONG . . . 153**

    I drop the need to be right and start questioning all my assumptions.

**CHAPTER 28: RECONCILIATION . . . 161**

    After not seeing my father for ten years, he visits me in Amsterdam and we reconcile.

**CHAPTER 29: I FIND MY SOUL MATE . . . 167**

    I meet Rani from Indonesia. I see that I am a better person when I am with her. We move in together.

**CHAPTER 30: SHEDDING MY SELF-IDENTITY . . . 171**

    Cees breaks down my self-identity in the harshest of ways. The experience is so overwhelming that I am bedridden for three days. In the process, I lose aspects of my self-identity, and it feels like experiencing death.

**CHAPTER 31: LEARNING TO LOVE AND ACCEPT UNCONDITIONALLY . . . 178**

    After trying to change Rani, I learn to accept and love her just as she is.

**CHAPTER 32: SEEING MY FATHER . . . 184**

    I have one last chance to see my father. We experience a deep connection. It's the last time I see him.

**CHAPTER 33: ANOTHER PROFOUND LOSS . . . 188**
Shortly after losing my father, I lose my mentor, Cees.

**CHAPTER 34: FINDING MY PLACE IN THE WORLD . . . 204**
After losing Cees, I must rediscover my gifts and decide what I want to do with the rest of my life.

**CHAPTER 35: DISCOVERING MY GIFT . . . 212**
I become a business consultant with a radical approach.

**CHAPTER 36: THE PARADOX OF MY WORK . . . 218**
In my work, I constantly struggle to find the best way to support people. More often than not, what they need is at odds with what they think they want.

**CHAPTER 37: CASTING OFF CHAINS OF SELF-IDENTITY . . . 222**
Learning how to allow parts of us to die before our actual death is one of the hardest journeys to take.

**CHAPTER 38: HAPPINESS CAN'T BE FOUND . . . 232**
The ideas we have about happiness are often what inhibits us from experiencing it to begin with.

**CHAPTER 39: ACCEPTANCE AND VULNERABILITY . . . 236**
When we allow ourselves to be vulnerable with our pain, it opens the door to a depth of connection and intimacy with ourselves and others that can be found in no other way.

**CHAPTER 40: YOUR LAST LETTER . . . 240**
Think of the person whom you love the most. Now imagine you have one final opportunity to say what he or she means to you.

**CHAPTER PHOTO INDEX . . . 244**

# THE SUMMER DAY

by Mary Oliver

*Who made the world?*

*Who made the swan, and the black bear?*

*Who made the grasshopper?*

*This grasshopper, I mean—*

*the one who has flung herself out of the grass,*

*the one who is eating sugar out of my hand,*

*who is moving her jaws back and forth instead of up and down—*

*who is gazing around with her enormous and complicated eyes.*

*Now she lifts her pale forearms and thoroughly washes her face.*

*Now she snaps her wings open, and floats away.*

*I don't know exactly what a prayer is.*

*I do know how to pay attention, how to fall down*

*into the grass, how to kneel down in the grass,*

*how to be idle and blessed, how to stroll through the fields,*

*which is what I have been doing all day.*

*Tell me, what else should I have done?*

*Doesn't everything die at last, and too soon?*

*Tell me, what is it you plan to do*

*with your one wild and precious life?*

# WELCOME

*"The secret to life is to die before you die—*
*and find that there is no death."*

·ECKHART TOLLE

**W**hen people ask me what I do, the simplest, purest answer is, "I prepare people to die." I'm not talking about people in hospice care or people with terminal illnesses. I'm talking about everyone, at every stage of life.

I am a coach and mentor, but primarily a friend. I spend about six months a year traveling the world to work primarily with CEOs and what society would label as "people of influence"—the kinds of people you would find on magazine covers. I generally spend a week with clients, living in their home, dealing with marriage, family, and business issues. Usually, problems at home bleed into the office, so it doesn't make sense to separate the two.

When I explain what I do, I often get the obvious question, "What qualifies you to do this?"

My standard response is to laugh and say, "Nothing—except that I've done it for the past ten years."

My work always comes from word-of-mouth, based on people's experience with me. My wife tells me I have been retired since she met me when I was thirty-seven years old. Her definition of retired is never doing anything you don't want to do. Based on that definition, I certainly agree with her.

I am quite intentional about how I perform my work. First and foremost, I am myself. I say everything that's on my mind—and I do mean *everything*. I share my observations, without reserve or applying a value judgment. At the same time, I am deeply principle-driven. I make my principles explicit so everyone can freely test them for themselves.

I do all of this while staying emotionally connected. I do not teach. I learn with my clients. I never ask anyone to do anything I'm not doing myself, or am unwilling to do—including breaking down in tears at what may seem to be inappropriate moments. My willingness to be completely vulnerable with clients comes from accepting my own pain. If I had to state the one thing that qualifies me to do this work, it would be my willingness to allow myself to be present, with the depth of all of my emotions, without fear, shame, or guilt.

In essence, I have turned my pain into my strength and made a "business" around it.

This book is my story about *how* I learned to face my deepest pain, accept it, and allow it to guide me in creating a meaningful life. And in my story, I believe you'll find reflections of your own story, and glean lessons that will help you create your own meaning in life.

I grew up with an abusive father and an unconditionally loving mother. My mother was my rock, my safe place, my source of emotional connection. She was killed when I was eighteen years old. That indescribably traumatic experience set the context for the rest of my life. I spent years trying to numb myself and run away from that pain. What I eventually discovered is that, no matter where I went, my pain was always with me. There was no escape. Eventually, I had to face my pain and ultimately, learn to embrace it. When I did so, it became my own greatest teacher.

From my observations of others, I know I'm not alone in running away from pain. I've observed that much of what people view as the "pursuit of happiness" isn't a pursuit at all. Rather, it's an attempt to escape pain. The irony is that in running away from pain, we simultaneously push away joy, peace, love, and connection—the very things we want most.

After thirty years of traveling the world and living in seven countries in search of happiness, I have realized that we humans are all very much alike. We all laugh and cry, celebrate and grieve over the same universal things. We all yearn to be seen and valued. We all ache for genuine human connection. We are all doing our best to make sense of this crazy life.

And in the middle of it all, we run into one of life's greatest paradoxes: It is precisely in our suffering that we find peace and the understanding of our universal humanity. That's where we truly see each other. That's where we can hold each other in compassion.

Yet in spite of this, we constantly find ways to avoid and escape the pain, heartache, and uncertainty of life. We escape into addictive substances and behaviors to distract us. We escape into TV, materialism, and partying. We escape into workaholism, achievement, obsessively climbing the corporate ladder. In short, we do anything and everything but allow ourselves to face reality and feel our real emotions.

As I said, I've been a master of escape myself. What I discovered is that, when I stopped running away from my pain, I was able to learn from it. What if suffering isn't there to plague us, but rather to teach us? As long as we run away from it, it can't teach us what we need to know to find peace. A meaningful life is not found beyond suffering, or in spite of it. Rather, it is found precisely in it and because of it.

For much of my life, sadness sabotaged and crippled me. But I've slowly learned to transform sadness into vulnerability and then action. I am often confused when I hear someone say, "I don't feel like my life is meaningful," which is usually followed by a discussion about what they do for a living and what they think needs to change. My thought is, if you want a meaningful life, simply consider everyone whom you love in your life and the fact that they may be gone tomorrow. Sit with that fear and vulnerability.

When you fully embrace this reality, it can become not something that cripples you, but rather something that motivates you. You can leverage that vulnerability into a meaningful life by following what it prompts you to do. For example, you can look at someone close to you, realize he or she will not always be there, and say simply, "I love you." In vulnerability we find connection, and in connection we find meaning and joy.

There's nothing more meaningful than sharing an open-hearted moment with another person, shedding tears together, truly seeing one another. But strangely, we instinctively, habitually, and expertly move away from these moments. We think we're avoiding pain, but in the process of avoiding pain, we're also suppressing joy.

When we learn to open up to vulnerability and accept reality as it is, instead of feeling something meaningful occasionally, *every* moment in life becomes meaningful. Our meaning in life is no longer defined by our job, our income, our status, our level of comfort and security, or anything outside of ourselves. Rather, it is defined by our relationship with and acceptance of reality as it is. Life no longer is a problem to be solved, but becomes a mystery to experience openly and fully. We no longer strive to get somewhere, for we realize that we are always here, right now. There's nowhere else we can go and nothing else we can do that will be any better or more meaningful than what we're experiencing in this moment.

True freedom can only be found by accepting reality as it is—even and especially when it's painful. The more we run from pain, the more we're enslaved by it. Pain is not a malicious enemy to be conquered, but rather a loving friend to surrender to. Pain teaches us to open our hearts to love and compassion.

I share my journey as it happened, uncensored. I have often felt that writers do a great job of sharing insights that come as a result of a long journey, while leaving out the messy parts—the parts that expose their humanity. I've written this book to show you that you are not alone in your messy journey. There is a wonder in getting it all wrong, only to realize that the apparent mistakes lead to the most wonderful discoveries.

My sincere hope is that my story will inspire you in some way to embrace pain and surrender to your reality as it is, with all the love, happiness, peace, and freedom that surrender brings.

## CHAPTER I

# THE DAY I DIED

It's a gorgeous spring Saturday in Irvine, California. I lace up my track shoes, put on my Sony Walkman, crank some grunge music, and start warming up. I'm competing in the long jump on the track team for UC Irvine as an eighteen-year-old college freshman. The field is large, the stands half-full of spectators.

I feel a deep sense of peace. I'm exactly where I belong, doing exactly what I am meant to be doing. I'm competing on a level I never would have dreamed possible a year ago.

My first two jumps are average, placing me below the competition. Before my third jump, I see my oldest brother out of the corner of my eye. I'm pleasantly surprised to see him, since he lives in San Diego, about an hour and a half south of here. I am not expecting him. We have grown apart since he left for college a few years earlier. He waves to me, but does not smile. I notice that he walks over and talks to my coach, but I don't pay attention because I'm focused on my event.

My third jump is better and puts me at second place ahead of three other jumpers. It's not the top spot, but I'm pleased to have placed. I always feel like I snuck onto the team, like I don't have the right to be here.

When my event is over, I run up to my brother and give him a hug. He is not warm, and looks at me solemnly. I ask him what he's doing here. He says he was just driving by and wanted to see me compete. He asks me to walk to his car with him because he needs to tell me something.

I say goodbye to my teammates, and we walk across the large fields adjacent to the track field. As we walk, I notice something in my brother's face I've never seen before. It is a dread that makes no sense—life is good and nothing can change that.

Or so I think.

A friend shouts to me in the distance, "Andy, I'll see you tonight!"

"Yes, I'll see you later," I shout back.

My brother says softly, in a strange voice, "No, you won't."

I'm confused. "No, we made plans so I'll see him later," I say.

"No, you won't," he repeats.

His next words change my life forever: "Mom died last night. She was hit by a drunk driver and was killed in the accident."

I lose all control of my body, as if I have taken a drug. I feel like I've been hit by a truck. My vision becomes blurred and everything goes quiet, as if my ears can't hear any more, as if they're protesting what my brother said and that if I can just block out the words for long enough, they won't be true. I fall to the ground in the fetal position and pound the grass over and over again in a mix of rage and pain. Tears stream down my face as I lose all capacity to reason. I feel pain and despair in a form and to a depth I never knew could exist. It is beyond words or explanation.

I have never felt or reacted this way before. My body and mind are completely disconnected. I am physically here and at the same time out of my body. Everything has slowed down. My brother speaks, but I hear nothing. There is a shallow humming noise in my ears. My eyes jump from place to place, looking for something solid to focus on, but everything looks foreign. I can't settle. I'm vibrating with emotion and my heart is racing. I'm not able to stand up. I am utterly incapable.

I flounder on the ground for what feels like an eternity. I don't care what people think of me. I have lost what I cherish most. I feel completely alone in the world.

My brother stands above me, embarrassed and not knowing what to do. Eventually, he helps me up and we walk to his car. I feel crippled. Each step is a labor. We get in the car and drive to San Fernando Valley to my mother's house, about an hour and a half away. It feels like an eternity. We drive in silence. No words need to be spoken. There is only pain.

I fiddle through his music cassette collection, looking for something to distract me from the agony. I see Don McLean's "American Pie" and put it in the cassette player. The lyrics of the chorus stab me in the heart:

> *The day the music died*
> *We were singin'*
> *Bye, bye, Miss American Pie.*
> *Drove my Chevy to the levee but the levee was dry.*
> *Them good ole boys were drinking whiskey and rye*
> *And singin' this'll be the day that I die.*
> *This'll be the day that I die.*

The last line echoes in my head. The song will haunt me for the rest of my life. Like an anthem for the pain, the words feel as if they were written for this very moment. I think, *This is the day I died*. My levee is dry. I am rotting inside and don't know how to express it. All of the wonder, joy, and opportunity I had felt prior to hearing my brother speak the words have vanished.

As I walk through my mother's house, an incredible eeriness weighs on me. I touch objects I know she might have touched a day earlier, knowing her hand will never touch those things again.

I have no idea what will happen to me from this moment forward. I'm not only in pain, but also thoroughly confused. All I know is that life will never be the same.

## CHAPTER 2

# DROWNING IN THE PAIN

**W**hile drowning in pain, I'm plunged into a strange process of answering logistical questions of how to deal with my mother's death. When do we get Mom's body? Where do we take it? When is the funeral, and who is going to arrange it? What are we going to do with her house and all her stuff? I don't want to think about any of these things, yet they become the most critical things I have to deal with. So, one by one, my brothers and I answer the questions, decide who will do what. I decide to write the homily.

I want to see her one last time, so we go to the funeral parlor. We walk into a cold room that is decorated with shades of brown, like something out of a 1970s catalogue. It smells like a hospital.

I walk up to the casket, which is surrounded by mountains of flowers sent by family and friends. It feels incredible to see the flowers because it is as if each rose is a word of loss felt by the person who sent it. In that setting, the flowers vividly show the magnitude of what has happened. Previously, flowers seemed arbitrary to me. Now, they have deep meaning. I see that this is not only my loss, but also one felt by the community.

There are also many cards. I pick up one that's from my friend, Tom. It is written to Mom directly, as if she could read it. It says, "Thank you for everything you gave me. I'm going to miss you." As I read the words, I am overwhelmed. It is as if I can't fully recognize the depth of my own pain until I see it in someone else. It is too close. I am frightened of what will happen if I allow my true emotions out.

They are reluctant to open the casket for us to see her, since she is so beaten up from the accident. As I look in, I see that the woman I knew is no longer there. Her face is covered with makeup. Even so, I can see the bruises underneath it. Strangely, it isn't disturbing because it is clearly not her. It's like I'm looking at a mannequin, some object that has been dressed up for presentation, without any sense of life in it. I touch her hand to make sure it really is her. It is cold and hard with no traces of Mom. No sense of comfort. No feeling of resolution.

The funeral is indescribably painful. Although I'm surrounded by hundreds of people, I feel completely alone. So many people tell me things in a feeble attempt to lessen the pain: "I'm sorry for your loss." "You must feel terrible." "She's in a better place." I feel the incapacity in all of these people who are doing their best to comfort me and not knowing how. I see that everyone feels the need to comfort me, yet they are so far removed from their own emotions. I need someone to break down in tears with me, someone to show me how to connect with my pain. Instead, I hear the same meaningless clichés repeated over and over again.

It all feels so inconsequential and even aggravating. All I want to say in response is, "You have no fucking idea." But I just nod my head over and over, in hopes that people will move on quickly. They can do little for me, and I do not want their sympathy. The church fills with hundreds of people, and with each handshake I feel more and more alone.

I realize that, from that day forward, I will never tell someone that I feel or understand his or her pain. Now I know there are some things beyond my imagination: the pain experienced by other people. You can see it, but you can't touch it. Anyone who tries just adds another insult to the actual pain. Now, when I see people in deep suffering, I quietly observe my own suffering and say simply, "There are no words."

I give the homily I have written to my cousin to read, because there's no way I can read it myself. As my cousin reads it, my throat feels incredibly tight, as if I have to swallow the sadness and my throat is fighting against it. It's so bad I end up with a sore throat.

In the homily, my words say that my mother's death will only mean something to the people in attendance if they live with a sense of urgency with those around them. I ask them to consider, "If you knew that the person you are sitting next to might not be there tomorrow, what would you tell them?" I have learned one of life's greatest lessons: I can no longer take anything for granted. Life is unpredictable. I see how oblivious people are to impermanence (just as I was before my mother died). Death, no matter how uncomfortable the topic may be, opens the door to an urgency to live. Yet all I see in people's faces is discomfort, denial, avoidance.

The whole process feels like a dream. I sit and observe the ceremony feeling a sense of dread and vacancy. I am there in body, but not in spirit. I am an emotionally stifled vessel in a room of social obligation. I walk from the church to the gymnasium where the after-ceremony is held for people to share their condolences. I stand in line shaking hand after hand, feeling nothing. The religious processions are all too much for me. I keep thinking to myself, "I've lost the person dearest to me. Can't you just leave me alone?"

I avoid looking into the eyes of the people who know me best, because I know they'll see through my façade. As each person leaves the auditorium, I feel the dread of my future looming. I don't have the slightest clue how I will survive without my mother.

During the days following the funeral I feel like an actor in a play. I am told what to do. There is a system to it, and I follow the well-worn path. We go through my mother's things and decide what to keep and what to get rid of. It all feels like an illusion to me because none of it serves a purpose now. I tell my brothers they can have everything. I don't want anything to hold onto because I have already lost everything. They don't feel good about that, so they put everything in storage, thinking that her stuff will be valuable to me at a later point.

I return to college to finish my freshman year, still in a deep depression. People tread lightly around me. I keep the same routine, but nothing is the same. I'm afraid to share the depth of my pain with anyone. If people really know the misery I am in, they might try to help me, which would force me to confront my pain. So I pretend everything is okay.

My friend Melinda calls me on the phone and asks, "How are you doing?"

My body tightens. My throat constricts. I tell her, "I am feeling sad, but I am okay." I am hoping she does not dig any deeper.

I am desperately trying to hide and it is not easy. I am constantly on the verge of tears and anything can set them off. I avoid too much contact with people because it is overwhelming. I can only pretend for so long.

Every night, I dream my mother is still alive. During the dreams, I'm flooded with happiness and love. Then I wake up to reality. The dreams are so visceral that I really believe she's alive and that her death is the nightmare. When I realize the truth, I feel like I'm getting punched in the stomach, and I break down into sobs. It's like reliving her death over and over again. It's torturous, and I start having difficulty sleeping because I hate waking up to reality.

I lose all faith in religion. I give up on everyone, including and especially God. God can't exist, I think, because he wouldn't take away the person who meant the most to me. And if he does exist, that would be even worse because, as I see it, it would mean my mother's death was intentional. So not only am I incapable of dealing with the pain, I am also unable to find hope or comfort in the world.

I go from an outgoing, fun-loving person to a hermit. I'm completely detached from life. My studies and sports become a refuge where I can avoid contact with others while appearing to function. I do anything so that people will stop asking me how I'm doing. I feel horrible and it's only getting worse.

I call my girlfriend and tell her, "It's over." I'm too emotionally shut down. I can't allow myself to be vulnerable. I can't bear being with anyone who might see or feel the pain that I am unwilling to accept.

She says, "We can work this out. I can help you through this."

I respond, "No, you can't. I need time to be alone." Deep down, I feel an addiction to the suffering.

Through this fog of pain, a glimmer of truth begins to emerge: This impermanent, fleeting life has no meaning unless we are able to share with others the full intensity of our vulnerability, pain, and love. And I have just lost the one person with whom I wanted to share my life. Now I am unable to find meaning in anything.

## CHAPTER 3

# THE RAGING MONSTER AND THE LOVING SAINT

I was raised on Cumpston Street, a cul-de-sac in Sherman Oaks, California. We were a typical middle-class American family. My father and my mother were both accountants until they started having children, at which point Mom became a homemaker. We lived in a Brady Bunch-like house with stonework on the outside, a fireplace, and a pool in the back. We had a dog named Apricot, a mutt with straggly hair. She was very affectionate and I loved her.

I was the youngest of three boys, and as a kid I felt like I had something to prove. I always got along with my brothers, but my brothers excelled in areas I did not. This would often get me into trouble because they would ask me to do things that would create havoc. For example, one time I grabbed a box of Rice Krispies. Instead of milk, my brothers convinced me to pour chlorine onto my cereal. I ended up going to the hospital. But my brothers were never angry or aggressive toward me, and I never felt any ill will towards them.

I attended a Catholic school, St. Francis de Sales, in Sherman Oaks. It was run by a staff of nuns and lay people. It was not a loving environment. The nuns were strict and our uniforms were a hard polyester material, which rubbed against my skin and made it hard to run around and play sports. When I was in eighth grade, one of the priests was caught sexually touching some of the altar boys. The priest was immediately sent to the Vatican, without repercussion. There was always a degree of denial that I could sense, even as a child. I was told never to talk about the incident or there would be trouble.

From a young age, I could run faster than most of the people around me, and I was proud of it. It gave me a sense of identity and security. I just wanted to be able to do one thing better than everybody else. I was given the nickname "Spaz" because I had difficulty remaining quiet and immobile, and had to keep moving all the time.

My parents divorced when I was ten. My mother went back to working as an accountant while raising us boys. My father was around, but he had severe emotional swings. Today, he would be diagnosed with a combination of depression, attention deficit disorder, and bipolar disorder.

As a child, I did not understand his severe mood swings. I was just deathly afraid he would flip and make me the object of his aggression. I blamed myself for saying things that would push him over the edge. So when his explosions inevitably came, I would think to myself, "You knew better." That feeling of blame would stay for a long time.

All this meant I became very dependent on my mom. She became the one person I could rely on. Our relationship was one of absolute trust and honesty. One time I brought home a horrible report card. She looked at it and said, "Andy, if that's the best you can do, then that's fine." She was always there to support the life I wanted to live without imposing her expectations on me. I would never lie to her. In return, she trusted me completely. There were only two rules: 1) never drive drunk, and 2) always use a condom.

My first major blow-up with my father happened when I was in eighth grade. My parents were divorced by this time, and a brother and I were at our father's house. We were all sitting at the kitchen table and he was asking us questions, in a weird way pushing us to be open. He almost gave me the impression that he really wanted to hear from us and improve things. I started thinking I could say what I really felt. In that vulnerable moment, feeling like I had a chance to connect with my dad and really be honest and maybe even improve our relationship, I told him I wanted him to be more like my friend's father.

When he heard that, he flipped and turned into a manic, raging monster. It was as if all his suppressed emotions from years came out. His eyes got big, he flailed his arms, he yelled and screamed. He raged about how horrible our mother was for turning us against him. He grabbed both of us by our collars, dragged us down the hallway, and threw us out the front door. I sat on the front porch and cried and cried. I remember walking home with my brother to our mother's house, in the middle of the night, tears streaming down my face.

At my age, I had no comprehension that such behavior was even imaginable. I never saw it in any of my friends' families. I realize now that that was when I started separating from my emotions. The pain would be so deep that I would put up walls to protect myself from my father. I wasn't even aware I was doing it. It was an unconscious habit I developed so I could survive.

Several months later, my mother, being the peacemaker she was, asked me to call my dad and apologize to him and make amends. So I did, and nothing was said about the argument or his behavior. There were no apologies or follow-up discussions. It was as if nothing had ever happened. And this happened again on many other occasions. It felt so wrong, and I was so resentful because I wasn't the one who needed to apologize. I have carried this resentment with me for much of my life.

Another time, when I was thirteen years old and my parents had been divorced for three years, my mother bought a greeting card for my father's birthday. She brought it to me and asked me to sign it. I just did what felt obvious to me and signed it with my first and last name, almost as if I were signing a contract. I didn't realize what I had done.

My mother saw it and said, "We can't give it to him that way!"

We immediately drove to the supermarket to pick out another card. I signed the new one with just my first name, but I spent the entire day wondering what the big deal was.

Fortunately, my mother was very loving and nurturing. She always compensated for my father's manic behavior by being my safe haven. I became very dependent on knowing at least one person was there for me.

When my parents split up, my father had hidden a lot of money so he wouldn't have to pay as much alimony. My mother did her best to raise us on a low standard of living. We moved three times over the next six years, each time to a smaller, more affordable place. With my mother working from nine to five, we didn't spend much time together. I became a "latchkey kid," coming home every day to an empty house and taking care of myself. But since I always felt loved by my mother, it wasn't a problem.

My two brothers excelled in school. They both ended up going to UCLA and became lawyers. I, on the other hand, was a slower learner. I often found that I needed to understand everything so completely that I was not satisfied with just memorizing a formula. I really needed to understand how that formula came into being, because my brain wouldn't allow me to assume that the formula was correct. This often meant that I would learn much more slowly. When I figured something out, I really understood it. But it took a lot of time, and I wasn't always patient.

My brothers also did well in sports, while, as always, I lagged behind. But that changed in my freshman year of high school when I joined the track team and committed to a single event: the long jump. In the middle of the season I asked the coach if I could also try the 100-meter dash. He said I would need to work out with the runners, but even then it would not be guaranteed. I worked out with the runners for three weeks. I believe the coach thought I would quit before he had to say no, but I didn't.

I was scheduled to run the 100-meter in our next meet. The week before the meet, I got teased a lot. Many of the athletes had seen me benched during the football season and did not believe I had a chance. The teasing only made my resolve that much stronger.

The big day came. I was anxious. I had spent weeks convincing the coach to give me a shot, and this was my only opportunity to prove myself. The gun rang out, and I ran faster than I ever had before. Each step felt as if it was propelling me to my place as someone who belonged on that field. It turned out that I actually did belong: To everyone's surprise, I won the race.

The coach ran up to me and told me I would be anchoring the 4-by-100 relay the following week. The feeling of gratification was overwhelming. Track had given me something I could not give myself: self-confidence. I was a new man. Carrying this track identity to the university was a big deal for me.

In my early years, I felt a constant tension between fear and love. The fear I felt of my father was in constant contrast to the comfort and love I felt for my mother. She was my rock. With her, I felt like I could achieve anything. I couldn't have fathomed life without her. But, as you already know, life had other plans.

## CHAPTER 4

# MY LAST LETTER

Thankfully, my grades were good enough to get me into UC Irvine. I didn't really know what to do with my life, but getting out of the house and experiencing life on my own was reason enough to go to college. I was feeling all of the intensity of it—the fear, the social pressure, the sexual tension. It was all there, running at full speed.

I found an apartment, which I shared with three other guys who had gone to a rival high school. It had two bedrooms, so we each shared a room. I ended up rooming with the pot smoker. Every morning I awoke to the sound of bubbles and the smell of marijuana as my roommate carried out his ritual of "wake and bake," as he called it. It was fine by me because I spent most of my time out anyway.

I had a dream to compete in track on the collegiate level. I didn't think I had much of a chance to make the track team, but soon after arriving I sat down with the coach, Kevin, to tell him I wanted to join the team and compete in long jump and the 100-meter dash. He told me they had no money for scholarships, but I was welcome to join the team. I was over the moon. I was given an opportunity to be something that mattered—a college athlete. I knew my chances of achieving weren't very high, but I was in the game, and that was all that mattered right now.

The first few months of college were dream-like. I floated from class to class, finishing each day with workouts on the track field. The sunshine always seemed to be out, and I was absorbing everything. Schoolwork was not neglected, but neither was it a priority for me. I was living out of my mother's house for the first time, and everything was exciting. I was let off the leash and it was time to run free.

After completing my first quarter of classes, I looked through the syllabus and one of the classes caught my eye: Sociology of Death. When I first saw it, my stomach dropped. Since about the age of about thirteen, I had been having panic attacks in the middle of the night. I would wake up and start hyperventilating at the thought of eternal non-existence. The thought that everything would disappear at some point paralyzed me.

No matter how hard I tried to conceive of a God, I was left with an empty pit in my stomach. I wanted so much to believe there was a God—anything to give me hope for an afterlife. But I saw that in order to believe, I would need to deny what my heart was screaming: "There is no god, Andy! Get over it!" My panic attacks would typically last five to ten minutes. Each thought heightened my fear, and it took time for the voices to settle.

These attacks came every two to three months. They were so overwhelming that, for years, I hid them from people. I had no avenue to share my anxiety because every time I did, people would try to solve it, as if there were a simple solution. I remember mentioning the topic to my brother who said, "You won't need to worry about it because you won't be aware of it anyway." Although the intent of the message was to assuage my anxieties, his words had the opposite effect.

Taking the Sociology of Death class would be an emotional challenge for me. But it was time to explore. As I sat in the fully-packed class, I realized the professor had gained celebrity status over the years. He was quirky and had a strange demeanor, almost like a caretaker at a funeral parlor who decided to teach instead of running a mortuary.

I began to examine the fear of death more closely. We read books by Elisabeth Kübler-Ross, the renowned Swiss-American psychiatrist who pioneered near-death studies, among others. I learned about the stages of death and, slowly but surely, questions arose about the meaning of life: Why am I here? If everything I know will disappear, what's the use?

I religiously attended class. I read all the curriculum and began to sense a deep need. I became more and more aware that eventually I would lose everyone I had ever loved. I would one day be nothing but a memory to the people I knew—and after those people died, I wouldn't even be a memory.

I felt helpless. The stark reality of mortality sat with me. As I sat with it, I started having more serious thoughts and asking serious questions. If all could be lost in an instant, then each instant we have is quite miraculous. Knowing I am going to die, how does that change things? How should I act differently? I pondered the things I had not done or said to people who meant something to me. I realized how infrequently I allowed myself the vulnerability of sharing love—it was easier to assume people already knew how I felt.

During one such reflection in my first year of college, a vision of my mother's face appeared to me. It was clear and honest and gave me goosebumps. I owed so much to her. I realized nothing was more important in that moment than telling her how I felt. Without taking a breath, I grabbed the closest piece of paper and began writing. I wrote the words that were most accessible to a still-maturing eighteen-year-old who was trying to figure out his place in the world.

*Mom,*

*I realize that I haven't always shared my experiences with you, like track meets in high school. I wanted you to know that this wasn't your fault, it was my own insecurity, but I have since grown and learned. I wanted to send this to you and tell you that I love you more than anything in the world. Even though I don't always tell you, I take it for granted that you know it. When I do well in life, I feel that much better because I know that you take as much pride in me as I do in myself. You have always been there for me and I don't know what I would have done without you. When I do well in school, track and life, I feel as if I'm doing it as much for you as for me, and that makes me happy.*

*Love,*
*Andy*

I held the letter in my hand and felt the tears of happiness flow down my cheeks. I was given a gift of this person in my life and this incredible opportunity to share what she meant to me. I saw the postman in the distance and ran to catch him in the hopes so I could hear my mom's appreciation as soon as possible. It was a beautiful day. I had reached deep into my heart and acted on the impulse that was speaking. I was full of life and I knew love.

A few days later I came home from classes and saw the answering machine blinking. I pressed the button, and it was a message from my mother. She said, "Thank you for the lovely message. I love you."

That night, just five hours after she left that message, my dreadful fear of death became a horrific reality: my mother was hit and killed by a drunk driver.

## CHAPTER 5

# A HOPE FOR PEACE

As my first year of college ended, I was still lost in a fog of depression and had no idea how to get motivated. Nothing that had inspired me before my mother's death interested me, not even the very things that had defined me up to that point.

I wouldn't say I have ever felt completely suicidal, but at this point it was essentially mental suicide. I was just a skeleton. Life was over for me. I had nothing to look forward to. I felt no hope, no joy. I was just going through the motions of life—and I really only did that so people wouldn't worry about me, because I didn't want to deal with their concern.

The best example of this was the Big West Conference track and field championships held in Fresno. I was, luckily, included on the roster to compete, which was an incredible privilege. I flew to the event on a wet and rainy day because I was scheduled

to compete against some of the best athletes in the US, some
of whom would become Olympians. But now, in the greatest
moment of my athletic career, I felt completely empty. I kept
telling myself, "Andy, you should be excited." But a bottomless
pit of grief soaked up any hint of happiness.

On that track in Fresno, I realized life is not about
achievement, but rather about sharing it with the people you
love. And I had lost the one person I wanted to share it with.

As if matching my mood, the weather only got worse. The
wind blew in all directions and the rain made sure that no one
would be able to get warmed up. But I didn't let that stop me. On
my first jump, I set a personal record. As good as it was for me, it
was well below the best of the athletes I was competing against.
But I had an advantage: I didn't care. As they struggled against
the rain and the elements, they failed to hit the mark, scratching
over and over again. With their ability, all they needed to do was
jog to the line, and they would have certainly out-jumped me.
But they were too focused on winning.

Strangely, I ended up placing in this competition, which
was completely unexpected for a walk-on freshman who had
just gone through the most traumatic experience of his life. The
amazing thing was that I did not care. It brought me no joy or
sense of accomplishment. The contrast between my feelings,
what this would have meant to me only a few weeks earlier,
and the empty reality at that moment, was excruciating. When
people congratulated me, I felt the same as I did when people
gave me their condolences at my mother's funeral. I felt dead
inside. My apparent victory was nothing but a charade and I was
a fool to keep it going.

At the conclusion of the track meet, I vowed never to set foot
on a track again. Whatever I had needed from track up until
then was no longer there. I no longer found any meaning or joy
in it. That experience made it so clear to me that everything we
value can switch in a moment when it is no longer meaningful to
us. I was now letting parts of my past die, and giving new parts
the opportunity to emerge.

During this time, I started noticing how aware I was of the
emotions of everyone around me. It was almost like I had been

given x-ray glasses for emotions. I was no longer listening to the words people would say—instead, I was now constantly observing the unspoken sadness, anger, frustration, or sheer denial of emotions. What appeared obvious to me was apparently completely unseen by those around me. I often thought to myself, "How can you not see this?"

It was as if I could just look at a guy and see he had been abused by his parents, and then immediately connect his behavior with that abuse. A friend would walk in the room and say, "I'm okay," and I would intuitively know he wasn't okay at all. Time after time, I would connect with people in ways they wouldn't have expected because they didn't know their emotions were so apparent.

One time I was hanging out with a group of friends on a Friday night. We were in our apartment living room, drinking beer, when one of our friends, Doug, walked in. Immediately, I felt a heaviness in him. He was slouching, his eyes were vacant, he wasn't smiling. No one else seemed to notice, but my mind was screaming that something was going on, and I couldn't understand why no one else was reacting to it.

I asked him how he was doing. He said "Fine" in a way that clearly showed that he wasn't. Not long afterward, everyone started leaving for a party. Doug said he wasn't going to join us. With my intuitive sense, I immediately said, "I'm not going either," making the excuse that I wasn't feeling well. I knew intuitively that you don't push people when they're dealing with something emotionally overwhelming. You let it unfold. So I just sat with Doug for about a half hour. Then I asked him gently, "What's going on?"

He broke down and told me that, just the night before, someone had jumped in front of his car on the freeway and he had hit and killed him. He went into great detail, telling me that parts of the man's body were still stuck on the front of his car. He couldn't get those images out of his head. We both cried and held each other.

This emotional sensitivity didn't feel like a skill, because it wasn't anything I aspired to have or tried to develop. I just couldn't turn it off, it felt almost like a superpower. I didn't find peace in this ability, nor did I nurture it. Just like my own pain, I pushed it away because it was uncomfortable—overwhelming, even. It wouldn't be until much later that I would fully appreciate the gift that we find in our own pain: compassion for the pain of others.

I was having trouble making sense of the world. My emotions felt so real, but the things I thought I saw in others were not reflected in their words. Emotions were not spoken about openly, but they almost always seemed to be the main issue in any situation. I was beginning to sense that there were two worlds: the world of everything we talk about on a superficial level, and the world of real truth where everything makes sense. Unfortunately, these two worlds seldom overlapped. My insight was already active in me at a young age, and had I coped with it by making jokes. I had become so adept at pointing out the pain that people were avoiding that my mother gave me the nickname, "My little shit-stirrer."

As I returned to college the next year, I started having trouble sleeping. Then I started seeing blood in my stool. Holding onto the pain of my mother's death was costing me not only my emotional health, but also my physical health. I had no idea what to do about it. The pain was like a bee constantly buzzing around my head. I was paralyzed by my emotions. My body was telling me something. The clues were getting louder, and avoidance was no longer an option. Fortunately, I discovered that the bleeding was only a fissure on the outside of my rectum. The doctor told me to drink more water and learn to relax.

I took the experience as a cue. I made an appointment at the school mental health clinic and began my journey into personal discovery. My first session at the clinic was scary. I was going to a psychologist to discuss a problem that I did not admit I had— namely, I could not process or accept the loss of my mother.

The psychologist was a young female graduate student who needed to build up credits through cases like mine. In an odd way, this made me feel a bit safer. I was less fearful that she would uncover the depths of my secret pain, which I was terrified of touching and exploring by myself.

She would ask, "How are you doing?"

I would respond, "Okay. A bit sad." I made sure not to go into detail.

She would always explore for more but I would share just enough to feel like I answered the question, without ever going into too much detail. She became exhausted with these efforts and suggested that we try hypnosis. I thought, "Why not?" As much as I resisted opening up, I did want to give it some honest effort.

On our fifth and final session, I lay down on the sofa and closed my eyes. She spoke slowly and gently, asking me to deepen into the experience. She instructed me to feel my body and let each part of my body relax. This went on for a few minutes as I entered a trance-like state. I never ended up being actually hypnotized, but I just felt at rest. My body was not tense, and I felt a release from the constant pressure. I had forgotten that my body could feel that way—without being in the vise grip of constant tension.

I saw the contrast—between what I had become and what I desperately wanted. I felt inner peace—one of the moments in life when you close your eyes and there is the deep sense that everything is exactly as it belongs. You are protected. You are loved. You are safe. You are cradled in support. It would take me decades to rediscover this feeling.

CHAPTER 6

# EXPANDING MY INNER AND OUTER HORIZONS

I entered my second year of college with a desire for more self-knowledge. I had made some great friends, but I felt like there was more for me than parties and studies. I saw my future: I could graduate, then get into the same routine bullshit life that I saw everyone else getting into. I could get into a corporate position and try to work my way up a ladder built by someone else. But I had no interest in that future. I felt a sense of dread in following a path that had been determined by others.

I was numb. All my sleepless nights had accumulated into a sense of delirium. There were moments of dread, waking up each morning, that I saw the prospect of dying as comforting. The thought that I would die gave me a sense of peace. I would no longer need to deal with my pain and confusion. I would sometimes hold my breath to see how long I could last, wondering if it might be possible to hold my breath until I died. I felt I had nothing to live for.

One morning, after one of my many dreams about my mother, I awoke. I was tired of feeling tired. I knew this way of living was not going to lead anywhere. I sat in bed for about an hour staring at the ceiling and wondering, "What am I going to do?"

Then, a thought caused a feeling to rush through me, as if I had been touched by a pulse of energy. I saw the possibility of freedom once again. The thought was, "When I'm dead and gone, none of this will matter. I will not matter. So why am I turning this into such a drama?"

If my life was already over, then why not commit suicide? I could metaphorically kill the person I once knew and allow someone else to emerge. Up until then I had mostly followed the wishes of those around me. But I could change my path. Instead of being the actor in someone else's play, I could write my own script.

Suddenly, I saw the world through new eyes. My senses changed. I felt a lightness I had never experienced. I was no longer attached to ideas about myself. There was still some shame and guilt in me, but I was less defined by them. I began to laugh at myself for being such an idiot. After living in a dark and musty cave, I saw the door open to a bright, new life. I felt incredibly curious to discover what a life looked like where I wasn't attached to societal standards. Who could I become now that I was no longer attached to the person Andy had been? It felt both scary and liberating.

At that point, I had nothing left to lose. I found a freedom in being and doing whatever I wanted without fear, to break out of social scripts and preconceived notions. My brothers were the high achievers who did everything the "right" way. I had always felt like the black sheep, but now I embraced that status with my newfound liberation.

The obvious question from there was, "If I'm free to do whatever I want, then what do I really want?"

That question, combined with the ever-present agony of my mother's death, set me on two journeys simultaneously—one external, and the other internal. The external journey was to break out of social scripts and pursue travel and adventure off the beaten path. The internal journey was much more difficult: to try to face my pain, to find meaning in my suffering, to make sense of what seemed like a pointless existence.

Although still burdened by deep sadness, I no longer felt attached to social norms. I no longer needed to please those around me in order to feel a sense of belonging. I was free to discover a new life, one that was no longer dictated by the past, one that could emerge without a plan or any idea of what the outcome needed to look like. I was given a second life.

From that moment on, the world changed. Every new day was a gift. I felt less attached to things. I started exploring in ways that I had never imagined. If I had died on the bed that day, then I would have missed out on the rest of my life. But I didn't die, I just left that person behind. He was not doing anything with his life anyway. I lost two of my close friends right after graduation—one was killed in a motorcycle accident and the other died from stomach cancer. I thought, "It could have been me. So why not just accept that it was?"

Up until then, I had been very shy with women. I was always fearful of rejection, so I would never ask anyone out. After my experience, if I found a woman attractive, I just said it. I didn't need acceptance, so I was no longer worried that I would be rejected. That insecure Andy was long gone. But at some point, I had shared with so many women that I found them attractive that it became a problem. On one occasion, I went to a party and a woman in a sorority asked me to her party. But another woman in the same sorority had already asked me to that same party. When I said I couldn't go, she got so angry that she poured a glass of beer on my head. We had not had a relationship before that moment, but for some reason she thought that we were already going out. I had been unaware that the ability to share your feelings with someone, without needing anything from him or her, actually made you more attractive. Who would have thought?

At this time I was also anticipating an end to my formal education and thinking, "What would be the wildest thing I could do to change my environment?" I began looking for ways to completely rediscover myself. Although I was not an arts student, I would sneak into pottery classes and make all sorts of pieces to explore my creativity. Since I didn't know what I was doing, I created a piece that exploded in the kiln, destroying all the pieces around it. When I arrived at class, I saw that everyone was angry about it. I pretended to be angry, too, so no one would figure out it was me. Although I was feeling more free, anger was still a difficult emotion for me to deal with. My father's explosions were seared into my mind.

I also picked up the saxophone to explore my musical talents. I lived on a small island near Newport Beach called Balboa. Taking the shuttle to the school one day, I sat next to my neighbor who was not aware that I was just learning the instrument. She assumed I was a music student. She spent the better part of the trip telling me how horrible her next-door neighbor was at music, not knowing it was me. She said, "Some people need to understand that they have no musical talent, and should move on with their lives." I couldn't resist telling her that the neighbor was me, and I laughed. She didn't.

I was beginning to laugh at myself without judgment. I was beginning to see that for years, my judgments towards myself had stopped me from exploring new things. Before, I was scared that I would be judged. I was worried I would be ridiculed for my lack of talent. Now, I relished the fact that I was actually trying something new.

The summer following my sophomore year of college I decided to leave Los Angeles so I could avoid living with my father. Instead, I went to Detroit, Michigan, to stay with an aunt who had married into wealth. My uncle owned several fabric factories in downtown Detroit, and he took it upon himself to give me a lesson in business.

That summer, he put me to work, for a short time, in each department in one of his factories. I worked in shipping, sales, logistics, quality control, and even at the dock to unload the bales of fabric. I loved all the different perspectives, and I wanted even more. I asked my uncle if I could work on the factory floor. This was the most dramatic and different place I could work. I was the only white person working on the floor with about 150 black, low-income employees who were living pretty rough lives. I wanted to feel close to an experience that I'd never experienced before.

I made two friends there, Tyrone and Marie. We would sit and talk on the shipping dock. It was often cold in the mornings. The smell of gasoline from the forklifts filled the air. The factory was busy and intense, and could be dangerous. There were fights and even stabbings regularly. I was a bit scared that people might see my privileged life and take it out on me, but it never happened. In fact, one of the men told me that most of the kids my uncle sent down from the family would just sit around and watch the others work, and he thanked me for my hard work.

Tyrone and I became quite close over time. One time we were talking and I told him that, growing up, I always knew I would go to college. I saw my brothers going to college. My parents always talked about college, and they even set aside money for me to go to college. I asked him if he ever thought of going to college.

He smiled and said, "Andy, I always knew I would never go to college. No one in my family has ever been to college. I never had any money set aside for me, and I never had the idea that could be possible for me."

That hit me really hard. In that moment, I realized that much of my life had been pre-determined. How much, I would never really know. What I believed to be "my choices" were just grand illusions—byproducts of the environment I was raised in. How much was I living someone else's dream? Did I even have free will? If I could no longer discern what I wanted and what part of my life was predefined, how many other things were predefined for me?

In light of all this, religion became a recurring struggle for me. I could not conceive of how a religion could punish someone in the afterlife if they were born in a country where that God or religion didn't exist. I began to see my life as full of stories that I had blindly accepted as true, completely ignorant of how they came to be. I wondered which were truly my ideas and which ones only appeared that way because I had not given them any deeper thought. As I have pondered this deeply throughout my life, I have been astounded by how scripted life can be for us, and how hard it is to break out of that scripted box and see life from a fresh perspective. It's nearly impossible to let go of the preconceptions and ideas that come with our culture and environment.

This new awareness, and the deep implications of it, began to grow inside me more and more. In a weird way, it felt like touching insanity. If I no longer could rely on the things that I thought were true, then I now had to find something new that was completely untapped before. This has become a lifelong pursuit for me—to explore everything from a blank-slate perspective, to examine everything I've ever thought to be unquestionably true, using fresh new eyes.

## CHAPTER 7

# VENTURING INTO THE OUTBACK

After summer in Detroit, I returned for my third year at UC Irvine, and I was ready for more experiences. I had learned there was much to discover and learn, and I wasn't going to do that by following the social scripts from the past. It was time to find my own path through virgin territory. After returning to school, one day I saw an advertisement for a study abroad program. I was drawn to the idea of putting myself in an entirely different environment where I could be anyone I wanted to be. I wanted to explore the world, as well as leave my past behind.

I debated which country to go to. Since I didn't speak another language, I was limited to English-speaking countries.

The choice came down to England and Australia. I wish I had better criteria for making the choice, but *Crocodile Dundee* was a famous movie at the time, and something about the outback drew me to Australia.

On my last day before leaving for Australia, my friends held a party for me. At the party one of my friends, Jonas, told me how much I meant to him. I was startled. He was so vulnerable, so honest and present in a way I had never seen him before. In that moment, I realized I had not yet mourned the loss of this phase of my journey. I was leaving a life behind that had taken years to build. I was leaving dear friends who had supported me. I felt sad and sick. I was leaving the security of the life I had known to venture into the unknown.

At that moment, I was unable to share the depth of my pain and loss with those friends. I was still shut down, unable to allow the pain to be shared. I could see the pain in everyone around me, but I was unable to express my own. Today, it is these moments that hold the most meaning for me. I allow this deep sadness to come out in the form of love and appreciation. It is in these moments that I feel closest to my heart.

But back then, my gut told me it was time to venture out into the world. It was time to test myself in a totally different environment and see who I was. I was happy to leave the pain of the past behind, as well as see what hope could be found in a yet-to-be-discovered future.

I arrived in Sydney, Australia on June 10, 1991. I remember this date because it was one day before my twenty-first birthday. I was disappointed because, in Australia, the legal drinking age was eighteen, so I missed out on the classic American experience of legally walking into a bar on my twenty-first birthday. That was something of a symbolic coming-of-age moment I had looked forward to from a young age. My travels would have to serve the purpose, I supposed.

Landing in Australia was a shock, but for reasons other than those I had expected. It was my first time traveling overseas and I was confused by how similar everything was. Outside of driving on the opposite side of the road and different electrical outlets, Australia wasn't that much different than the US. The real differences were less obvious, and it took me time to decipher what was really unique.

I was studying at Sydney University, which was like an Ivy League school for me. The buildings were majestic and they looked like the pictures you'd see of Harvard or Yale, buildings from the 1800s with a rich history. Stepping into the Quadrangle Courtyard was like entering a *Harry Potter* set. There was a mystical feeling about it all.

The first week after I arrived, I attended an orientation where I learned that nothing had been arranged for me. The woman in charge of the orientation looked at me and said, in a wonderful Australian accent, "Sorry, love, we haven't arranged any accommodations for you. You'll need to figure that out for yourself."

I was overwhelmed and had no idea where to start. But I also knew I had to buckle down and figure it out. So I ran around and found a place to live, a terraced housing unit with a typical Victorian front, three stories, and a metal black fence in front. There was a working-class group that had already lived there: a taxi driver, two bartenders, a waiter. They all shared this single building. I stayed on the bottom floor.

My housemates were polite, but not very friendly. They had rules, but those rules only applied when it suited them. Once I invited some friends over, and my housemates quickly said that wasn't appreciated. They didn't like Americans and our way of living, and they commented on it regularly. In reaction to anything they didn't like about Americans, they would often ask, "Have you read the book *How to Win Friends and Influence People*?" I always felt uncomfortable living with them. The taxi driver would often come home at night, drunk, banging holes in the walls and screaming at the top of his lungs. I'd sit in my room, scared, remembering how I felt as a kid with my dad, and never being quite sure what might set off an explosion.

I began noticing that, although I had grown older and moved away from home, my feelings from childhood remained the same. When I experienced angry people, I would immediately regress to the thirteen-year-old version of myself, to that moment when I was forced to walk home after telling my dad I wanted him to be more like my friend's father. I was afraid of that anger and I judged it. I wanted nothing to do with anyone who expressed anger. At that time, I was unable to see that the problem wasn't anger in others, but rather my inability to deal with it. But it would take me many years to fully embrace that.

I spent a lot of time working, often more than I studied. I didn't want to spend the money my father had saved for me. I wanted to be free to make my own choices without feeling any obligation to him. I got work through an outsourcing agency on campus that would send me to jobs where someone had called in sick. Every morning at 8:00 a.m., I would get a call from Suzanne: "Andy, you're going to work at the restaurant today," or, "You're going to work at the nurses' college today," or, "You're going to work at the fitting for graduation gowns today." Each day, I would go into a completely different job with a completely different environment and learn to adapt. It was quite remarkable.

One job was cooking in a restaurant. I was put on the job without any training. I was asked to cook steaks that day. I put ten steaks on the grill and was told to make them medium. I cooked them a bit too rare. They were all sent back at the same time. I put all of them back on the grill, but then forgot which one belonged to which person. It was a mess. I went back the next week and saw the cook I had replaced the week before. He growled at me, "You're the one who screwed up my business." I wasn't always successful, but I tried.

By jumping from job to job without preparation or training, I was learning one of life's most important skills: how to adapt. I saw that getting along with people was 80 percent of my work. The other 20 percent was skill. As long as I made sure relationships were healthy, I'd have the time to learn the skill. If the relationships were off, things did not go so well, no matter how good I was at the skill. So when I showed up for a new job, I did not pretend or try too hard. I observed and saw where I could contribute without getting in the way. I became someone people wanted to have around, so I continued to get more and more work.

I slowly built a group of friends. I began to notice the subtle ways people's approaches to living differed from my own upbringing. In the US, people were very quick to promote themselves and their achievements, while the Australians would do everything to downplay even the greatest of successes. I remember this most dramatically on display when a friend from my university in the US came to visit me and spoke with my Australian friends. When he left, one of my Australian friends remarked, "Andy, your friend is really good looking. Just ask him." It was this sarcastic, often self-deprecating humor that I began to understand and eventually deeply appreciate.

On the other hand, I also saw how the anxiety to self-promote could limit people in their desire to achieve. This was something the Australians call, "Cutting the tall poppy." If a person places himself above the group, their tendency is to cut him down to size. I found this curious as it began to remind me again of how our cultures define us. In this case, it was impossible to judge one custom as better than another, because in the society where it was created, it works.

With the backdrop of this social observation, I saw that looking out at the world could only get you so far. At some point, different electrical outlets, varying accents, and curious driving practices lose their charm and you are left with humanity. It was here in Australia that I started to see what made human beings so similar, rather than different. I began to see my own pain and loss in the broader context of humanity. I began to see that, in our desire to consider ourselves unique and special, we lose sight of the fact that we are all very much the same. This became apparent in the weeks that followed as I met people who would change my life forever.

## CHAPTER 8

# LEARNING TO LET GO

After nine months of studying at the university and living in my crazy house, I realized I needed to find a new place to live. The transition was made easier when I found my first real friend in Australia, and probably the first person in my life whom I could call a dear friend. This was a big deal for me. After my mom's death, making friends had been threatening because it opened the door to talks I did not want to have.

His name was Matthew. I met him through a mutual friend and we quickly hit it off. We moved into a little shop together as roommates. We covered the windows of the shop in black paper to have privacy.

We were both intellectual in nature and loved to discuss heavy-duty topics. We spoke long and often about the world and our place in it. Matthew had studied journalism and had written for *The Australian* newspaper. In his passionate desire to change the world, he had quit his prestigious post to study politics and the environment. His dream was to become a politician in Australia's Green Party.

He was important to me because he was the first person I could talk to who didn't stop with superficial cordialities. He would challenge just about everything I would say.

At first, logic dominated our discussions. We challenged one another and did our best to understand each other. We made definitive statements and drew firm conclusions. Although I was unaware of it at the time, this logical process was a way to rationalize my loss and the pain of it. I was trying to convince myself that if I could somehow mentally understand it, that would in some way alleviate the sadness. In other words, logic, like my travels, was yet another way to avoid facing my pain.

I spent the better part of that year learning to understand my emotions. To be more precise, it was more about controlling them. This all came to a head in one of my late-night talks with Matthew. Whenever I spoke of my mother, I would often speak in elevated and loving ways, so much so that she began to take on a saintly status. Matthew used this moment to confront this belief.

He said, "Your mother was no more special than anyone else. She was not a saint and treating her as such does not do justice to who she really was." I could see he wasn't trying to be insensitive, but simply challenging me with an honest idea. Still, his words were a complete affront, and they cut deep.

I responded defensively, "Maybe that's true. But I still love her."

"That's fine," he said. "Just know what you're really loving. Love what was really there, not a romanticized idea. Because if you romanticize and idealize her, you'll never get over losing her."

As I sat with this, I started connecting some dots. I realized that what I thought I was holding onto wasn't my mother—the raw reality of who she really was—but rather a conceptualized version of her in my mind. And if she was not the saint I had held her to be, then the pain of her death lost part of its stranglehold on me. I saw the addiction in pain. If we tell ourselves the same story long enough, we become addicted to its outcome.

The beliefs I carried about my mother had given me a sense of security. I needed that belief, because by believing my mom was an angel, I also could believe no one could replace her. Furthermore, by holding on to this belief, I would live in the constant pain of losing someone more special than anyone or anything else. And in this constant pain, there could be no progression, no moving on, no healing. Ironically, I had created an idealized version of my mother in reaction to the pain of losing her, but it only made the pain more intense and longer-lasting.

Most importantly, I saw that this romanticized story kept me away from saying the simplest, yet most painful thing: "Mom, I miss you."

Although I began to discover the power stories can have over us, I was not prepared to embrace the implications and accept it without reserve. To accept this, I would have had to make peace with more than what I was capable of at that time. I still had major issues with my father that I was running away from. Yet the levee now had a crack, and no finger was going to stop the rush of water that was building up behind it. It was just a matter of time.

As with all things that are strung together in reaction to pain, my logical arguments slowly unraveled. The contradictions got larger and the ability to hold the constructs together in any meaningful fashion became harder. The idea that intellectual understanding could connect me to a deeper healing in any way was beginning to crumble.

In the wake of this struggle to actually feel my emotions and not rationalize them, I made an incredible discovery. Until that point, my life had been a constant escape from pain, either by shutting down emotionally, shutting off close relationships, or running away to Australia. I was still using my travels as a way to distract myself from my pain. Subconsciously, I was training my mind to protect my heart. I was convinced that simply understanding emotions intellectually was the same as healing.

Nothing could be further from the truth. I was packing more and more dirt on a pile of pain, hoping it would go unnoticed. The outcome was emotional "dirt" in the middle of everything—my friendships, my love interests, my family. In every contact with others, my primary goal was to avoid discussions about my emotional dirt. Yet the dirt was right in front of me and impacting everything. Rationality allowed me to talk about the dirt pile—without having to feel it. I could go into my head, and I could pretend that it might go unnoticed.

Matthew asked me once, "How did your mom's death impact you?"

I answered in a way that, to the blind eye, might appear that I was emotionally connected. I said, "It changed everything. I lost my inspiration. I lost any real sense of passion. I lost my home."

What I was unable to say was, "Each day is torturous. I lost the person who meant most to me. I don't know if I will ever love again. I'm in pain. I'm suffering. Will you hold me?"

Because I was not able to share these words, I lived in fear that they might one day come out, and that my secret would be exposed. If any discussion turned too emotional, I checked out. In suppressing my emotions, I restricted the intimacy of my relationships with others and became more detached and intellectual.

Now I had taken a step—I was no longer stuck in bed. But I was far from happy. I still had a lot of emotional work ahead of me. Yet, true to form, when I could not solve my emotional issues, I turned to adventure. I again asked myself, "If you had nothing to prove and no one to please, what would you do?"

A smile came across my face as Mike Dundee's face reemerged in my head and I heard him say, "G'day mate." I decided I was going to work and live in the Australian outback. How, I had no idea. But I was certain I was going to do it.

## CHAPTER 9

# LIFE AND DEATH
# ON A RANCH

S eeing my schooling in Australia coming to an end, I realized I still wasn't ready to go home. In a chance meeting with an Australian friend, I learned that there were ranchers looking for "jackaroos," or ranch hands, for the summer. I immediately jumped at the opportunity to postpone my return to the States.

I sneaked into the agricultural department one day and asked where I could find a list of farms throughout Australia. I was not exactly sure what I was looking for, I just knew it needed to be somewhere in the outback. I wrote down fifty farm addresses, by hand, and went home to write a letter to each ranch. I just needed one to say "yes." It took about two weeks to receive the first replies.

One morning I got a phone call from someone whose accent was so difficult for me to understand that I thought it was a practical joke. I did my best to answer quickly so my friends wouldn't laugh at me afterwards. After asking all my friends, I found out the call was genuine.

A few days later I got a call from Robert Bomford, the owner of Cotswold Ranch. He said he was the father of three sons and would be happy to welcome me into his family for the summer, on one condition: that I spend time speaking with his children about my life. Robert was originally from England and he wanted his children to have a better understanding of the wider world. He told me, "I have lived around the world, but my children have not had that opportunity. I'd like you to spend time with them so they can see life from your perspective."

So I spent the next three months discovering life on a sheep and cattle farm. The location was everything I expected. The nearest neighbors were a half-hour drive away. You could drive around for hours and never leave the property. The vast space, miles away from the nearest neighbor and full of thousands of sheep and cattle roaming around, created for me an entirely different perspective on life.

In this isolation, I again began to wonder, "What if I had been born here? What would my life look like? What opportunities would I have? What would I possibly miss out on? And what makes this life any less special or relevant than any other life?" These were the same thoughts and feelings I'd had with my friends in the Detroit factory, and now these thoughts were surfacing on the other side of the world, on a quiet farm in the Australian outback.

Waking up on the farm was a dream come true. It was one of those very rare occasions when imagination and reality line up in a perfect union. The house was so old and in such bad shape that it should have been torn down. It was not built on a solid foundation, so pieces had sunk into the ground. None of the doors closed properly because the doorframes had all twisted through the years. There was no heating other than the fire in the kitchen, so we huddled on cooler nights and went straight to bed. Then every morning I would wake up, go outside, and pee on the grass. I didn't know pee kills grass.

At one point, Mrs. Bomford asked angrily, "Who is peeing out the door?"

I sat quietly hoping to avoid her condemnation. Feelings from my relationship with my father were triggered. I never peed on the grass again.

The lifestyle was completely foreign from everything I had ever known. It was challenging. I felt so alive with the experience. I wanted to experience everything there was to do.

We woke up at around 8 a.m. and divided our time between building fences, shearing sheep, and fixing anything that had gone wrong the day before. It was the start of sheep shearing season, so we took the dogs out to round up all the sheep. After they were herded into the pen, we put deworming medicine in their mouths, cut off their tails, and put rubber bands around the males' scrotums so that the testicles would eventually fall off.

I noticed the Bomford family seemed a little skeptical of me because of my city upbringing. That changed one day, though, about three weeks into my stay. We were building fences, and part of the job requires using a mechanism to stretch the barbed wire and tighten it before connecting it to the post. As I was stretching the wire, it snapped and part of it flew back into my leg. Several pieces of barbed wire stuck into my calf. I looked down in surprise, unable to process what had just happened.

I looked at Robert, and then said in a calm voice, "Hey, Robert, can you come over here?" He came over and saw the wire stuck in my leg and was surprised by how calm I was. He grabbed the wire with pliers, counted to three, and yanked them out all at once. I bit down and accepted the pain. He smiled at me, as if to say, "Now you're part of the team."

On the farm I saw a fine line between life and death. I saw the cycle of life in stark and grisly detail. I had always bought prepackaged meat from the store, and now I saw where meat really came from. On Christmas we had a pig to butcher. A neighbor, skilled in butchering pigs, came over to help. He took one pig from the pen while the others squealed bloody murder. I felt a deep sadness hearing it.

He jabbed his knife into the pig's throat and the blood

streamed out. He tied the pig's feet together, then pulled up until it was hanging in the air. I wanted to cry but it was not the time or place. They sliced the pig along its belly. I was asked to remove all the guts. I sunk my arm into its body cavity and tore out all of its internal organs. The organs slipped through my fingers as I tried to drag them from the carcass to a plastic bag. I pretended it didn't bother me. I was the outsider and I felt as if I had something to prove. The odor of the pig was impossible to remove from my skin and clothes. Afterward, every time I would raise my fork to my mouth, the stench would be right in my nose. I was unable to eat much for the next week.

It was truly disgusting. I wanted to punish myself for participating. Yet I also felt a sense of responsibility for doing it. I had eaten pork many times throughout my life, without having to face my victims. I had spent weeks feeding that pig before helping to kill it. Now I was beginning to see the disconnect between the meat I ate and the beautiful animal it came from. It was so much easier to grab meat at the supermarket. I did not need to consider that that pig had a name and a friend that was left behind. I was not going to turn into a vegetarian, but at the same time, I was not going to hide from the knowledge that something had to die for me to have that meal. In ordering meat on the menu, I now embraced the consequences.

But in the act, I also saw the interdependence of all things: how death is necessary for birth, how this pig's death sustained my life. It helped me to begin seeing that death was not a tragic misfortune, but a part of the process of life.

One time we were driving and spotted a kangaroo, which is considered a pest on Australian farms. Trying to gain acceptance from the family, I shot the kangaroo and killed it, only to find that it had a baby that was still alive. My heart still sinks as I recall looking at that baby kangaroo whose mother I had just killed. I was told that, as an act of mercy, I would need to kill the baby. I couldn't do it. I was sick to my stomach. One of the boys I was with eventually picked it up by the tail and slammed it against the ground.

I have to live with this image the rest of my life. I shot because I wanted to fit in. I wanted to be accepted. I wanted to tell a story.

I live with the fact that two innocent animals were killed for my social desires.

Yet I no longer defined myself by my mistakes, but rather how I dealt with them once they were made. In these moments, I saw the potential to transcend predetermined societal norms. I was free to stop behavior that no longer suited me. I saw that there was a cost to trying to fit in. I could just say no, and there was a freedom in seeing that I could experiment and learn. I could create my own future, without judging the decisions of others.

One of the best days of my life was New Year's Day, 1992. The Bomfords had a horse that was very seldom ridden. I had asked for weeks if I could take him out. This day I was given permission. I took him out at sunrise and rode for hours. I was alone in this vast land with only a few kangaroos and rabbits to keep us company.

I was enveloped in the environment. In the vastness of the outback, I felt how small and insignificant I was. I felt at one with nature, with nothing to distract me or draw me away from myself. I was fully alive. A deadly brown snake crossed the grass in front of us. This could have turned ugly, but in my present state, I calmly moved the horse in a different direction and we went on quietly. It felt like every being was in the place where it belonged, and I had no reason to overreact. I eventually returned to the farm feeling a deep sense of peace.

As my time at the farm came to an end, I realized I was more emotionally sensitive than most of the people around me. I was living from my head to protect myself from my deep well of pain. I had no idea what would happen if I were to let the floodgates of my emotions open. What I did see is that nature was important for my well-being. If all my feelings could be encapsulated in a single beautiful sunset, what need was there to talk? No words were needed in the face of such indescribable beauty. Nature can speak to us in ways that the rational mind might not understand, but it is more powerful than any words spoken. In those moments of peace, I could just let it in.

I also saw two contrasting parts of myself. I loved to be with people, and at the same time, I loved being alone. I saw that there was a peace I could only find in quiet moments. The fact that I was alone in the world no longer felt sad to me. I was beginning to see that we are all alone in the world. Instead of the fear that would often arise, I was beginning to feel peace in my solitude. I knew I had a long way to go before I felt a deep, lasting sense of peace within myself, but I was starting to sense it. I was finding moments that pointed me in the right direction.

My trip to the outback was complete. I had experienced everything I wanted to do and feel here. I was now at a crossroads. I was supposed to go back to the US and finish my final year at university, but my heart was not in it. I was ready for another adventure. This time, I wanted to do something even more drastic.

## CHAPTER 10

# GOING WALKABOUT

One of the things I really enjoyed in Australia, and everywhere else I've traveled, is trying on different perspectives of living. In Australia, the perspective that touched me most was this idea of "going walkabout." The term originally referred to indigenous male Australians embarking on an extended journey as a traditional transition into manhood. But it has evolved to refer to any Australian youth traveling for an extended time, typically during college years.

Australia is far away from the rest of the world. It's a twenty-hour flight from Sydney to New York, for example. So when an Australian goes away, his goal is to spend as much time as possible traveling because it takes so long and costs so much to get anywhere.

A lot of my Australian friends at that time would talk about what they were going to do after graduation. They would often say they were going to take a year or two off from school and travel the world with a backpack. It sounded incredible to me. What I found even more remarkable was that it was a cultural norm. It was almost expected that people would spend these long durations of time traveling, experiencing and enjoying the world.

I asked myself, "What if I could embrace this part of the Australian culture and make it my own?" Since my time in the factory in Detroit, it was becoming increasingly apparent how much my life was influenced by my upbringing. I saw there was a freedom in being able to take aspects of another society and apply them to myself. What I found great in this culture was the lust for life and experience. I was not going to let that opportunity slip through my fingers.

When my stay at the ranch concluded, I determined to do my own walkabout. I planned to take a year off from school and travel the world. The world was at my feet, and I had this incredible opportunity to just explore. I could really experiment, and experience and test my ability to grow and adapt. It felt amazing.

I called my father to tell him I had decided to delay my last year of college to take a year's sabbatical to travel the world. He started raging, shouting over and over, "You finish what you start! You finish what you start!" He screamed as if he said it long enough, I would somehow relent.

I responded that I was still planning on finishing my degree. But he wouldn't accept it. Our relationship had always been adversarial, and my decision only made it more so. Over the years I would share less and less with him and, in return, he would get more and more angry. But now I was independent.

I hung up the phone feeling overwhelmingly frustrated. I was not seen by my father. I was not understood. These were the feelings that had built up for years. I felt helpless to do anything about them. I wanted his respect, support and love. Unfortunately, I only felt looked down upon by him—like a young misguided child who, he believed, was wasting his life. These feelings only strengthened my resolve to lead my own life. So I ignored my father's wishes and his anger and turned my focus to travel.

This was in 1992. I had no Internet or mobile phone to guide my journey. I only had a *Lonely Planet* guidebook. My original plan was conservative: I would spend a year roaming around southeast Asia. That changed after a chance meeting with Alexei Mazin, a friend of a friend who had done a lot of traveling himself. When I shared my plan with him he looked at me with disdain. He said, "You have a year to travel the world and you are going to waste it in southeast Asia?" I tried to convince him there was enough to do there to keep me busy for a year, but he would hear nothing of it.

Alexei saw me as a project. Every time we would meet he would plot a new destination for me. He would say, "Andy, if you are going to visit Thailand, then you've got to visit China." I would do my research and add it to the list. Then a few weeks later we would meet again and he would say, "Andy, if you are going to China, then you must go to Russia." This went on for weeks until I finally ended up with an ambitious plan that would take me overland, from the deserts of Australia to the Red Square in Moscow.

What Alexei helped me discover is that by trusting others, I could go further than I could go alone. Allowing this trust was new for me, and dredged up a lot of fear in me. But in that trust, I saw it was possible to take risks. And it was in those risks that I made my greatest discoveries. I was grateful to Alexei for helping me see that, by opening yourself up to the ideas of others, you can create something far greater than you could have ever imagined by yourself.

In February of 1993 I set off for my first destination, the island of Bali. When my flight landed, I was welcomed by sights, sounds, and smells I'd quickly get accustomed to: congestion, hawkers, and the smells of burning trash, humidity, and fried food. Several hawkers tried to get me into their taxis and take me to the best and cheapest places to sleep. I loved it. I had no clue what I was doing, but I had a riddle to solve. How do I get to the hotel and spend the least amount of money?

I'd often struggle with three or four other arriving tourists to find the local bus so we could save a few dollars. It became a game—how to survive without getting ripped off. We were so preoccupied with not getting taken advantage of that we would often spend an extra two hours to get to our final destination. But as far as we were concerned, we beat the system. We didn't end up seeing much because we were so busy planning each leg of our journey. But we were happy.

In general, I kept a low profile during my travels. I would always buy a book on the history of the location I was traveling to. I often felt like it was an extension of my education abroad. I could often find a small group of people to travel with. It made planning easier and it usually kept costs down to share the costs for rides. I was a butterfly who went with the rose that smelled sweetest. It was all so easy.

It was also cheap. Since I did not have high standards, I could pay as little as three dollars a night for accommodations at cheap youth hostels. I would also travel primarily with the locals. I found that even if it took a bit longer, I got to truly see the country while riding next to the live chickens that were being brought home for dinner. The US dollar was strong at the time. As long as I stayed in countries with relatively weak currencies, I could stretch out my travels longer. I only needed about $1,000 per month to survive, which included flights. And because I had worked and saved, I had plenty for the trip.

In some cases, I pushed the limits of trying to stretch my money. One night I slept in a hut on the beach. When I woke up I found that all of the leather on my shoes, which had been two feet from my head, had been eaten by rats during the night.

This time was filled with deep personal reflection. I would write in my journal on a daily basis and crystallize the important moments from the day. I did not follow the path to beaches and recreation areas, but rather to villages and points of interest. I very rarely had a plan before arriving at any destination. I let the momentum take me.

I very seldom said no, although on some occasions I should have used better judgment. While in Thailand, the family I was staying with was very welcoming and invited me to join an outing to collect frogs during the rain. We left at 11:00 p.m. as heavy rains hit. As the frogs jumped out of their holes that would fill with water, we would grab them and throw them in a bag.

To make sure everyone stayed awake all night, we were given some form of "speed" in the form of a pill to keep us awake. I refused at first, but as the people I was with insisted, I tried to break a part off and hide the rest. I took this homemade drug and did not sleep for the next three days. My entire system was jacked with energy. It was so intense that I had to cut my trip short and fly to Hong Kong for medical help. Trying to adapt and learn had its limitations.

I happened to be in Indonesia during their election season. Each day, a different political party was allowed to conduct demonstrations in the streets. My idea of a political demonstration was very different from what I saw in Indonesia. As I walked around, people trickled out onto the streets until there were masses of people, all waving the color of their party with an intensity that verged on anarchy. The processions moved in, their trucks stuffed with more people than they could fit. The screams got louder, the eyes got larger.

That day I followed the crowd to the main square, along with three other foreigners. The idea of seeing a political rally in a foreign country was exciting, but as we walked to the square, we could feel something was off. There were no other foreigners around, so our presence was very obvious. When we arrived at the square, I saw four towering structures that had been built for the event. Taking a closer look, I noticed snipers atop each of the ramparts, looking down on the passersby.

I was just starting to realize that my desire for thrills could turn dangerous. As soon as I felt the desire to leave, two armed men approached us. They spoke very little English, but they commanded us, "Come!" One of the people I was being taken with was an Australian surfer. He continued to say how cool the experience was, completely ignoring the potential danger. We were escorted about 300 meters away to a small building where we were asked to wait. We sat waiting in that room for forty-five minutes without knowing why we were there.

Then the door opened and three men entered. One was clearly a high-ranking official, another turned out to be a translator, and the last was one of the officers who had brought us there. The official asked us, "Are you journalists?"

The Australian, still caught up in the adventure of it all, said, "Yes, we are student journalists."

I was shocked. I jumped in front of the Australian and said, beating my chest, "Me tourist! Me tourist!" The official saw the fear in my eyes and clearly understood. He said some words in Indonesian and we were escorted by the same two officers back to our holding room. The Australian laughed the entire way back. As for me, I was reminded how fragile life was. I would need to be careful about whom I traveled with, given I could not assume that others would be using good judgment.

My lust for life had the potential to become an addiction to adrenaline. In looking for bigger, better experiences, I was ignoring the potential risks. The high came from thinking I'd have a great story to tell afterwards. I was trying to create moments, instead of just being with the moment. This constant search for adrenaline highs was unsustainable.

Although punctuated by these occasional off-the-track adventures, my travels became surprisingly routine. I jumped through Indonesia and into Malaysia and Thailand. Since tourism was so popular in those countries, there was relatively little adventure. It felt more like an extended holiday than a journey.

The more I traveled, the clearer it became that I was not alone on my journey. Just about every traveler was carrying the same *Lonely Planet* guidebook and following the same recommendations. We were all heading in the same direction. Like it or not, we often formed a group by default. So after weeks of this routine, I became disenchanted: There was always a McDonald's or Kentucky Fried Chicken to remind me that the world was already quite globalized, and finding magical hidden spots was not easy.

The excitement I began the trip with was slowly turning into routine: open guidebook, select next destination, travel, find accommodation, repeat. At some point, it began to feel like a job. I was getting numb.

There was an aspect of expectation that became more and more apparent to me. In my search for adventure, I made assumptions of how it would look. When the journey became tamer than I had expected, I lost my original interest. Thus, my expectations were dominating my life by determining my attitude. I was looking at things the way I thought they "should" be instead of enjoying them just as they were.

This process of being disappointed in my own expectations became a riddle. If I had no expectation and just showed up, then everything would be marvelous. But the fact that I imagined how it would be meant that I no longer enjoyed it. So now I needed to go to more and more countries to satiate my desire for "special" experiences.

One night in the youth hostel, I was sitting next to a German man who handed me a pencil. He asked me, "What do you see?"

I answered, "A pencil."

He laughed and said, "Yes, but what do you see?"

I looked again and began to describe it. "I see yellow. I see a dent. I see the name of the brand."

He asked again, "What else do you see?"

I saw that my mind was looking for things it could name. For specific parts of the pencil.

He pressed, "What else do you see?"

To look further, my brain had to shift the way it looked at the pencil. I was no longer focusing on the details, but rather sensing the whole.

I said, "I see the tree the wood came from to create the pencil. I see the factory where the paint was made. I see the planet where this object exists. I see the universe where that planet is located." I went on and on.

What I realized is that, the moment I thought I knew something was the moment I lost curiosity. But by looking at everything with new eyes, a beauty arose that carried me into a beautiful space in my mind. In this space, I didn't make assumptions. Rather, I was continually open to exploring. I was releasing my mind from the need to know.

I was beginning to see that my happiness was very much connected with how I looked at the world. Happiness, I saw, is not a place outside of myself, but a place I found inside myself. I still wasn't clear on the connection between expectation and happiness. But I could not deny that there was a relationship. I saw that the more I relaxed my expectations, the more I saw the world through the eyes of a child. The more I entered my journey with expectation, the more I sat in judgment of how it was "not as good as" or "different than" or "uninteresting." I saw how my mind wanted things to be a certain way. It was constantly imposing expectations onto the world. When my image did not match the reality, I got stuck.

I was not able to completely stop this from happening. But, with practice, I started noticing it more and more, and so it became less and less dominant. I was able to see that I was more than just my thoughts. I was beginning to learn how to alter my thinking, and with that, my experience of the world.

While coming to grips with this new reality, I had a surprise ahead of me that would challenge everything I thought I knew.

## CHAPTER II

# EXPLORING CHINA

I n China, *everything* was different—from the food and clothing to the language and customs. I felt like I had entered the Twilight Zone. The year was 1993 and China's great economic growth had not yet begun. There was very little tourism, and few people could speak English. Anyone who could speak English was frightened because of the Tiananmen Massacre just three years prior. Since then, speaking with foreigners verged on treason. There was no Coca-Cola or McDonald's. We had no shared cultural heritage. I began to feel as an explorer might feel first landing and then trying to communicate with the natives.

I found in China the confusion and wonder I had been missing. This did not come without hassle. The simplest tasks became tiresome. In my first week in Canton, I went to a street vendor to buy nuts. I had been so accustomed to gesturing for things

I wanted that I took it for granted that people would gradually understand me. I raised my index finger and pointed to a bag of nuts, mouthing the words, "one." I was met with a blank stare. I raised my finger again, this time more obviously, then pointed to the nuts. The man looked at me as if I had just asked him to kiss me. His eyes got big and I had the distinct impression that he had never interacted with a foreigner before. I felt helpless. The more I would point and make mouth movements, the less he understood me. It turned into a drawn-out Abbott and Costello comedy routine and I ended up walking away without my nuts, but was beginning to feel nuts.

Eating became its own adventure. There were no menus in English and speaking was not an option. So I would walk into the kitchen of each restaurant and point to ingredients, smile, and wait for acknowledgment. In the end it all worked out, but I could not take any social norm for granted. And after visiting the meat market in Canton, I resolved to be a vegetarian. I saw lots of animals in cages, including dogs and porcupines, which made it clear I could not trust what would be cooked for me.

While I was in China, my old friend Alexei suggested that I go visit his friend in Wuhan, a city off the beaten path. I thought it would be nice to finally speak with someone local. I had been there for three weeks and had not really spoken with a single person, outside of simple greetings.

I arrived at Wuhan by train and I was told I would need to book a ticket back to Beijing immediately, as it could sometimes be difficult. I went early the next morning to find long lines of people in front of windows that were three meters high and painted black, top to bottom. At the bottom of each blacked-out window was a tiny hole. You couldn't see the person on the other side unless you tilted your head against the counter to look in the small crack. It was as if people were hiding their identities to escape retribution for what they were going to do to you.

I went to the counter and requested a ticket to Beijing. I was told, "Meiyou." I had heard that word several times and knew it meant, "No."

I was stunned. I was given no further instructions. I was shooed away. I came back the following day only to be treated the same way by a different attendant. When I went home and explained this dilemma to a fellow traveler, he laughed at me and said, "You have not figured out how to get things done here. You need to go to the counter and yell at the top of your lungs until someone gives you what you want."

I thought the suggestion was insane, but I also didn't have any other viable option. So I went to the counter the next morning and asked again for the ticket to Beijing. Again, I was summarily rejected, as if I were an inmate looking for a pardon. Then I did what felt like the unthinkable: I screamed as I had never done before. I made a scene that would make a toddler tantrum look mild. I kept yelling, "I want one ticket to Beijing and hold the Meiyou."

It was a large station and there were a few hundred people roaming around. When they saw this foreigner yelling, it was like a comedy routine for them. They laughed and pointed at me as if to say, "He finally figured it out!" I stayed at the counter for several minutes. Although the line behind me was growing, I didn't care. I kept on yelling until a supervisor came to inform me that I would need to come back tomorrow. But he did promise me a ticket.

Although the next day I still did not succeed in getting the ticket, I did raise the attention of those around me. One man with a soft smile told me he could help me out. He told me to arrive at the station fifteen minutes before departure and he would get me on the train. He gave no details. I was a bit nervous, but again, I couldn't see an alternative. I met the man at the station and he took me through a dark corridor under the train tracks. In the corridor, I began to wonder if this was smart, but eventually we came out next to a train platform, a place you could only reach with a ticket. He placed me on the train and said, "When they ask for your ticket, tell them you lost it."

Again, short on options, I played along. When the conductor came, I explained the situation. He repeated several times, "How could you get on the train?" I acted ignorant and prayed that he was not going to throw me off. He did not. I paid for the ticket and learned that resolve has a way of making sure you get where you need to go. I was so busy trying to get the ticket that I never met the friend I had gone to visit.

I made it back to Beijing. I felt a deep sense of gratitude for the young man who had helped me without asking for anything in return. When I offered him money, he had smiled at me and said, "Just enjoy your trip." This act of kindness left me feeling overwhelmed. I was in a terrible spot and someone I didn't know made this effort.

To this day, I still feel like I'm repaying this favor. When I'm walking the streets of Amsterdam and I see someone in distress, I always ask if I can help. Just recently I was in a shop and a glass cabinet fell over onto a child and cut his head open. The parents didn't know what to do. I took the boy and his father on my little moped to a local hospital. He was overwhelmed with appreciation, just as I was the day I left the station in Wuhan.

Sometimes you wish for something, and once you get it you see that it's not what you thought it would be. I entered China looking for an experience where all my assumptions would be challenged. The experience of being unable to get a ticket out of Wuhan was exactly what I had wished for. What I neglected to consider was all the conveniences I assumed would be present. By actually getting what I wished for, I was pushed to the limits of my frustration and incapability.

I became free when I embraced my frustration and started yelling at the woman at the ticket counter. I was laughing at myself for getting exactly what I wanted and seeing that the joke was on me.

After arriving back in Beijing, I hopped on the Trans-Siberian railway to Moscow. It takes six days to cover the 8,986 kilometers (5,623 miles). Entering Russia was an interesting experience for me. For one, it had been the home country of communism. But secondly, it was the home of my family name, Chaleff. The Chaleffs were Russian Jews who had immigrated to the US some three generations earlier. Although I did not have a connection with any family in Russia, I had a deep curiosity about where my ancestors had come from.

I shared the train with a curious mix of traders, travelers, and tourists. The highlights of the days were stopping at train stations and picking up supplies. As soon as the train came in to the station, we would hang out the window to buy from the people shouting out what they were selling. There were always hard-boiled eggs and cheap tennis shoes.

I found the economics of the people on the train very curious. Many merchants were using the train to transfer their goods throughout Russia. They would drop off a box of something at one location and pick up a box of something else at another. It was a well thought-out process of continually upgrading goods until the final destination, Moscow, was reached. I have always been fascinated by history, and this reminded me of the shipping routes during Holland's Golden Age, where a trader would bring salt to trade for other spices, which were then traded for other items at the next location.

On the trip, we stopped for two days in Mongolia. Hawkers on the train asked to exchange currency, and offered to sell odds and ends to the travelers. One of the hawkers became so insistent that I thought the only way to discourage him would be to play around with him until he got annoyed and left. He shoved money in my face and yelled, "Exchange! Exchange!" I asked, "How much?" Regardless of his answer, I would say, "That's not enough."

The game went on for a few minutes until he'd had enough of me. He pulled out a knife and raised it menacingly. A few people jumped between us. The angry hawker ran the knife across his neck to threaten me. I traveled in fear for several hours afterward. I was humbled to realize that what may appear as funny could be potentially deadly. On another night, a man tried to force his way into the cabin I occupied, reaching his arm in through the crack in the door to see if he could grab something.

I spent a few days each in Moscow and St. Petersburg and loved them both. I had been away from the US for almost two years, during which time I had had very little contact with my friends and family. I hadn't returned home for a holiday or a special event. It was now time for me to return home. "Home" had always been a hard word for me. After my mother died, I lived in many places, but none I could call home. Home was no longer a location for me, but rather a state of mind.

The irony of travel is that you go out into the world to discover the differences, and you come to discover how similar all people are. If there is one thing that the years of traveling taught me, it was that we human beings share more than we could ever imagine: our hopes, fears, and aspirations. I was no longer seeing myself as an "American," but rather as a citizen of the world. When people criticized American politics or economics, I felt less inclined to defend my home country, or agree with them. I just so happened to be born in America, as someone else happened to be born in Australia, Japan, or Finland.

The more I have traveled, the more I have realized that the ultimate journey is not outside us. It is inside ourselves— an endless journey of discovery that is as beautiful as the most beautiful scenery.

The monotony of travel taught me something magical. A life of exploration gets old if you are looking to discover something outside of yourself to make peace inside of yourself. I was no longer looking to visit monuments. Instead, I was wondering how places would move me. Did I feel closer or farther away from my emotions while I was there? Did I discover something about my assumptions about what is "normal"?

What became most clear to me was that travel could not pacify the pain of the loss of my mother, or help me face the fear of my impending contact with: If I kept moving, so the psychology went, the sadness wouldn't have an opportunity to catch up. I certainly did not understand the depth of my pain, nor the journey required to find peace again.

Yet I had no time to think about that. After two years of absence, I was heading home.

My mother and father.

Clippings from the newspaper after my mother's death.

Competing in the high school long jump.

Our childhood dog, Apricot.

Me and my brothers.

Going away party to Australia.

My terrace house in Australia.

The Sydney University Quadrangle.

Working in the graduation gown
department at Sydney University.

Alexei giving advice on my travel plans.

Matthew standing in front of the blacked out windows of our house.

The house on the Cotswold sheep and cattle farm.

Giving birth on the farm.

Gutting the pig on the farm.

Polical rallies
in Jakarta.

The meat markets in China.

A market in China.

My graduation.

# CHAPTER 12
# LEARNING TO QUESTION MY THOUGHTS

I arrived back in the US one day before my college classes began. It is often said that the shock of traveling is nothing compared to the shock of returning. This was certainly true for me. Coming home was returning to a place that was familiar, and at the same time, totally foreign. Most of my friends had graduated during the year I left for Australia. I felt very lonely at first, so I had to reconnect with what school meant to me: after spending a year traveling the world, I had come back with an entirely different perspective on things.

I was a different person, yet I found myself back at the same place I had started. With all my friends gone, it was both a blessing and a curse. I did not need to break any old patterns and, at the same time, I was blown away at how I was no longer interested in things I had valued before. I did not want to go to social functions and campus events. Still, I was excited that my second time around at the university was going to be different.

I had a degree in social ecology, which was vague enough that I could take some really interesting classes. And after having all of this experience traveling, I felt as if I was ready to take on the world. I sat in on Ken Chew's demography lecture and loved it. I asked odd questions and challenged every assumption I could find. After class, he would often rush out of the lecture hall in fear that I might catch up with him to ask hard questions.

It was incredible to appreciate school for the first time. I had always been a just-above-average student, and now I had become a straight-A student. I never realized that all those years, I had just been bored. I always assumed I wasn't smart enough.

I would call this time in my life the Age of Intellectualism. I felt cosmopolitan and sophisticated and wanted to share with anyone who would listen. I would speak about art with my roommate, John, who would look at me with a mix of boredom and disdain. Eventually, he would leave the room saying he had to study, just to avoid continuing the discussion with me.

To satiate my new desire for learning and be more constructive with it, I decided to take a philosophy course. This course was taught by one of the most dreaded professors on campus, Dr. Raymond Novaco. He was a thin, commanding man who took karate and survival training on the weekends. He was the type of person who, if you said something in class, you'd better be prepared to answer the next question he would ask which was usually: "How could you know that?" He asked that question so often that students were brought to the verge of tears, thinking their lack of preparation might be exposed.

What I learned, in this mix of fear and intellectual stimulation, was that our thoughts are just that—thoughts only—until we understand what they're based on. Speaking without critical thinking just fills the air with noise. For the first time in my life, I was actually thinking instead of defending my opinions and biases.

For that class, we read one book per week, which was never easy for me because I had a hard time sitting still. Eight of us sat around the table reflecting on what we read. I would share diligently what I took away from the book. I was often frustrated by my colleagues' lack of preparation and caring. They usually had not read the book, yet they would often share opinions so strongly that it was impossible to open a dialogue.

I realized that thinking is much more challenging than simply having beliefs and opinions. I no longer accepted letting my brain run free without checking the quality of the content.

It was in this relationship with Dr. Novaco that I learned to look beyond my thoughts, and start to see things with increasing objectivity. I saw that I was inclined to certain beliefs—but just because I believed something didn't necessarily make it a fact. I would need to begin to explore things more deeply in order to feel confident in anything I had to say. The question I started asking myself was, "How did I come to think this way?" This is as opposed to, "How can I prove this point?" This first question initiated an inward journey of curiosity and discovery, while the second would inevitably result in frustration and conflict.

Throughout my life, I have tended to find people to replace the love I did not receive from my father. Ray was the first male figure in my life to fill this need. I was unaware of it at the time, but I needed the masculine energy of a father, without the anger. In this relationship, I discovered that it was possible to develop a respect, and at the same time, love. There are times in life when you need someone to give you the confidence you cannot give yourself. One of the most incredible moments of my life was when I recently went back to visit the school to see Ray with his students and he said to them, "I'd like to introduce you to one of the best students I have ever had." To this day, it brings tears to my eyes.

Soon after I returned to California from traveling, I received a call from my Aunt Ann. She was a wiry, spunky, opinionated Jewish lady going on eighty who always seemed to know the right thing to say. She was worried about my travels, so she began to share her concerns. She told me that running away from my problems was no way to solve them. If I truly wanted to live a fulfilling life, she counseled, I would need to confront the pain and not run away from it.

I knew she was right, as she often was. But I also knew something about traveling made me feel alive. The thrill came from placing myself in a foreign environment to test myself and see who I was. I agreed with her, but then asked her, "Is there anything in your life that you regret not having done?"

She admitted, "Yes."

I responded, "I won't."

The dynamic of our conversation immediately shifted: before, I was a child with an adult, and now we were two equals, just two people enjoying one another's company and appreciating one another's beauty. Still, something in me knew she was right and that eventually, I would have to face my pain once and for all. But I still wasn't ready.

I wasn't in the US long before setting sights on my next adventure. I was nearing graduation and had no idea what I was going to do afterward. What I did know is that I wasn't excited about starting a formal work life. I was working part-time in the Travel Abroad Program office on campus. My job was counseling people who were considering the possibility of studying overseas. At the same time, I applied to UC Berkeley for Demography because after so much traveling, I was intensely curious about the social and economic development of cultures. I wanted to study how cities take form, and how group consciousness creates shared understandings of the world. Unfortunately, my math scores weren't high enough to get me into the program.

One of the programs I helped students with in the Travel Abroad office was called the JET (Japan Exchange and Teaching) Program. It was unique in that it set up qualified individuals from English-speaking countries to find employment in Japan. Although I was not interested in the program for myself, Sean, a friend in the office, needed a ride to his interview. I had a car so I drove him to the Japanese consulate.

I thought it wouldn't hurt to have an interview myself. I was curious enough to check it out, and I was also just covering my bases. It felt like I was throwing a bunch of cards in the air and seeing which ones would land face up. I walked in with Sean, and was interviewed by a white American man. He asked me basic questions about my history and fear of being away from the US for an entire year. As I had already spent two years outside of the US, it was clear that I was not a major flight risk. About a month later, I received an official letter informing me that I had been accepted into the program. Unfortunately, Sean had not made it in.

I was starting to find comfort in the spontaneity of my life. Just like with my travels, during which I awoke every day and decided where I wanted to go next, life was beginning to unfold easily and spontaneously. I did not need to have a master plan. The universe was planting seeds at my toes. Instead of looking up at the stars in confusion, I could look down at my feet and see what was right in front of me. I felt some fear and anxiety, but I continued to remind myself that life is short. I did not ask myself, "What am I going to do next?" Instead, I asked, "What do I want to do?" I felt the excitement in my belly and realized, "Wow, I am excited."

While in the US, I spent very little time with my father. He was still angry that I had taken the year off to travel. When we did see each other, he reminded me of his disapproval. I was excited to show him that I had gotten straight A's, but he paid no notice. It was no secret that he did not approve of my life.

Once, while sitting at the same table where we'd had our violent confrontation a decade ago, he demanded, "Why don't you become a lawyer like your brothers?"

I sat quietly, avoiding any hint that I heard him. This avoidance only got him more frustrated.

"When are you going to stop wasting your life away?" he said, trying to provoke me.

I walked away, feeling sad and rejected. My need to feel appreciated by him never ceased. On my graduation day, he pointed to my diploma and said, "With that piece of paper and a dollar, you can buy a cup of coffee." It felt to me like every moment that I wanted to share with him was destroyed because I was not the son he wanted.

I was left with the option of going to Japan, or trying to find a job and not knowing where to start. I opted for Japan. After less than a year back in the US, I would be leaving again for a new adventure. I purchased some language books, but otherwise I was wholly unprepared for the adventure before me. Although I had been to Asia, Japan would be different. It would challenge my self-identity on the most fundamental level.

## CHAPTER 13

# A CLASH AND A CONNECTION

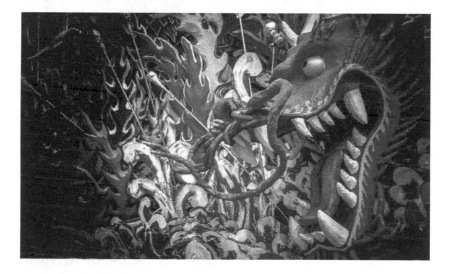

**A**s I landed in Tokyo, I immediately felt Japan was different than anything I'd experienced up until that point. So many things made no sense to me here. People would bow at what appeared to be arbitrary moments, and papers would mysteriously change hands.

Before arriving, someone told me about the importance of business cards in Japanese society. After that, I was never to hand a card to another with one hand, nor was I ever to receive a card from another with one hand. The rule was to use two hands and make a slight bow as the other receives your card and returns with theirs. In Japanese society, there were a lot of those types of rules. Following the rules was not the problem, but

79

trying to understand why these rules existed in the first place was a challenge that would preoccupy me over my two-year stay.

All the JET participants were shuffled to our respective towns. I was sent to a small farming town called Shinjo, where some of the country's best rice was produced. I was greeted at the train station by Uematsu Sensei, who would be my direct superior at the school where I would be teaching English. Being my direct superior meant he was responsible for my well-being. He was also responsible for any mistakes I might make while I was in Japan. He was very scared that I would do things that would create a problem for him.

The first night, Uematsu took me to a traditional *ryokan*, or inn, where we had a traditional Japanese meal together and he introduced me to Japan. He was very cautious to make sure I was comfortable. He always looked at me with questioning eyes, as if he were wondering what I was doing, almost as though he had never met a foreign person.

That night, we were served a soup I had never seen before. In the soup was what appeared to be a massive shrimp with an armor like exterior. I looked at the exoskeleton and I was in utter awe that the Japanese would eat that. But I thought, "I'm here, so I'm going to jump with both feet into the water and fully experience Japan." So I put the shrimp in my mouth and started to chew on it. It crunched in my mouth and was terrible. Shell splinters were tearing my mouth, cutting the insides of my cheeks. As I chewed, I thought, "How strange that they eat this."

Then Uematsu said, "Do you eat that in your country?"

I looked at him in surprise and said, "No, we don't."

He was very concerned because he hadn't protected me by explaining that I wasn't supposed to eat the shell. So he took the same shrimp that was in his own bowl and ate it with the shell on. I asked him why he was eating it, and he just nodded his head and didn't say anything. I saw that he felt an incredible responsibility for me. That turned out to be both beautiful and problematic during my two-year stay. He was almost like a father who wanted to protect his child from doing anything wrong, knowing the child would never be able to take responsibility for the consequences of his own actions.

Shinjo had one major street that ran to the train station. My small, one-bedroom flat was about 100 meters straight out the door of the train station and to the left. My apartment block was named Mezon Shinwa, which was the Japanese spelling for "Chinese home" in French. Inside, it was typical Japanese. There were two tatami mat floors, and sliding paper doors to separate the bedroom from the living room.

The house was heated by a gas stove that sat on the middle of the floor. It was completely detached from everything so it could be easily moved anywhere. It was quite dangerous as it emitted fumes that would fill the air, which often gave me headaches. To get fresh air, I had to open the door, which meant the room would get cold. It was a constant struggle balancing the heat. So I purchased a uniquely Japanese invention: a very low table with an electric heater attached to the bottom, facing downwards. During the winter, I'd sit for hours on the tatami mat under that table, often sleeping there to stay warm.

Even with all of these quirks, and often because of them, I felt completely at home. It was the first time in my life that I was living alone in my own apartment. I had a full-time job teaching English at a local school. I was learning the ins and outs of a culture that was foreign and interesting.

One day my neighbor, Miyu, showed up. Miyu was a beautiful Japanese woman with four children, which was quite rare for a Japanese family. She invited me to have dinner at her home, which I gladly accepted. The kids were incredibly excited to see a foreigner walk in the door. I did magic for them, which I had learned from my brother, a professional magician. But when we sat around the table, it was apparent I was missing something. An older gentleman in his eighties, who had burns all over his body and could barely walk, sat with us, quietly observing all our activities.

From the first moment I met Miyu, I saw a pain and a deep sense of longing in her eyes. I learned she was the owner of the one and only bookstore in the village. Miyu was known in the city because of the family business, of course, and also her artistry as a pianist. She had been a child prodigy who travelled around the country and became quite well known. But Miyu was also the only heir in the family. So, in spite of her love for music, she was required by the family to give up her piano career and have a family. She found a man who dropped his family name so she could carry on the Yamada name.

That night, when we finished eating and all the children went to sleep, Miyu and I sat at the kitchen table. I asked her how she was doing. She said it wasn't easy for her. I asked, "What isn't easy for you?"

She explained that just two years earlier, my predecessor in my job had visited her at home. She was so excited that she forgot she had left the tempura on the stove. The oil in the pan caught fire, and the house, full of combustible materials, burned to the ground in minutes, along with the shop below. Her children were saved. But the rest of her family was not so lucky. Her grandmother died in the fire, while her father received horrible burns over 80 percent of his body. To invite me into her home was incredibly emotional for her.

She told me that in Japan, fires were seen as a violent offense to the neighbors. A fire doesn't just risk your own house, but also the livelihood and property of everyone around you. So the Japanese treat the one who started the fire as a pariah. Miyu told me that, as she sat on the street crying as her house was going up in flames, one of her relatives started shouting angrily at her. I could see in her eyes that she hadn't healed from that experience.

We spent the next couple of years healing together. I could see that, for her, our relationship was an opportunity to reconnect to the things that were emotionally important for her. We spoke just about every other day. I had dinner at her home three or four times a week, and the kids became like brothers and sisters to me. We spoke often about the emotional journey of her giving up music and accepting the family life. And she would always get emotional when she spoke about music. We would look into one another's eyes and see each other's pain. I saw in Miyu a sadness, like the sadness I was unable to resolve in myself.

I asked her if she wanted to play music with me, because I was a few years into the saxophone. She said, "Yes, I'd love to." I started bringing my saxophone with me to her house, and we would play all the jazz standards. She was incredibly talented, so she usually played around my mistakes. I saw that this gave her a sense of closure around her decision to give up the piano to carry on the family name. She would often tell me how appreciative she was of helping her find the pain and accepting that it was okay, and that she was loved for who she was, in spite of what she had done. She lived with devastating guilt.

Miyu was also very much a caretaker in the typical Japanese sense. She would bring me miso soup when I was sick and gently remind me of things that I was unintentionally doing to cause offense in Japanese culture.

In Miyu, I found someone who could recognize my pain, someone I could be there for and with. Each of us had a rough history behind us, and we were like two alcoholics trying to stay sober—or, in our case, not let depression overwhelm us. I began to feel how close two people could be in silence. I learned how to sit with my thoughts and allow myself to be seen. We did not need to heal one another. Just feeling seen for the first time was something quite dramatic. There was nothing romantic about our connection—it was a pure human connection in mutual compassion.

Miyu was never ready to say what was on her mind. So I would often have to stop speaking and wait until she was finally ready to share. She was always worried she would offend me. When she felt comfortable, she would often correct me when I would speak. It was clear she was sensing something I was not able to see. She was grounded in a humility I did not understand.

I would always speak from the "I" perspective and I could see that it made her uncomfortable. For her, and for everyone in her culture, everything was seen in terms of "we." One night I was speaking highly of something I had achieved in the school where I was working. She cautioned me, "See the achievement that the school has made possible for you. See how you are only part of that achievement." I was always cautioned to think in terms of the group consciousness and not my own.

She would guide me in ways that didn't always feel comfortable. Although I was learning a new language, what she was teaching me was beyond language. It was a deep sense of being in the world, a shared consciousness that we are always part of a bigger whole, that our success and achievement is bigger than ourselves. I was learning a humility I had not yet fully grasped. I slowly began to let go of something that was important to me—the part of my identity that was individualistic and wanted to feel unique and special. In Japan, individuality was not only unwelcome, it was actively discouraged.

I struggled with my individuality. There was a space in my brain that wanted to be seen as unique and special. I wanted to feel the sense of accomplishing things on my own. I wanted to be proud of my achievements. I wanted to prove my worth to myself, as well as to my father, whom I could never impress. Who would I be without that pride? I would have to let go. I saw that sometimes, ideas can propel us forward, but then become limitations. I had defined myself through the Western mindset of valuing individuality. Now it was time to feel the beauty of a whole different way of being in the world, where my individuality was less important than the health and well-being of the community or culture.

I started coming to grips with the intersection between Eastern and Western culture. The West was about personal development, success, achievement. The East was about inner peace. I began to see the yin-yang nature of our existence and the fine line between outer achievement and serenity. It was a balancing act that would take me years to see in myself and hold in my consciousness. To this day, for me it's still a balancing act between two very powerful and loving friends that complement one another at the best of times, and struggle against one another at the worst.

CHAPTER 14

# CONFUSED BY COMMUNAL RESPONSIBILITY

After a year in Japan, the most I could express in Japanese was common greetings. I rarely understood what was going on. So I decided to take a class to learn Japanese.

I moved to Tokyo, a few hours south of Shinjo, to go through a month-long language immersion course. A friend's family graciously welcomed me into their home and gave up one of their two bedrooms for me. The house was just forty square meters and there were six of us in the house. Five of them were sleeping in the other room. The room I slept in was used for eating as well. It was very uncomfortable displacing the family. But I was learning to accept the amazing generosity of the Japanese people.

They also fed me every day. Every morning was a traditional Japanese breakfast, including rice with *natto*, a traditional fermented bean that has a strong taste that even many Japanese cannot bear. I always ate everything, and the hosting mother, Aiko, was continually impressed that I never complained about food. Every morning I would tell her, "Oishii," which means "delicious."

My class was on the opposite side of the city. Summers in Tokyo are sweltering hot, and the daily subway journey is an exercise in patience. As rush-hour commuters squeezed into the train, I let my mind wander to someplace other than the man's underarm that was squashed against my nose.

The class began every morning at 8 a.m. From the moment students entered the room, only Japanese was allowed to be spoken. All instructions were given in Japanese and replies were only accepted in Japanese. The day was broken into two parts: 8 a.m. to 12 p.m., and 1 p.m. to 4 p.m. There were about fifteen other students from around the world, and we all felt overwhelmed.

The class started with the teacher, Nayoko, asking us to conjugate verbs. We sat in a circle and each person was asked to conjugate a verb in past tense. I struggled with Japanese grammar. In my head, the word order was clear: subject, verb, object. As in, "I went to the market." Yet in Japanese I was forced to allow my brain to speak a sentence and not know the tense until after the verb was spoken. So instead of saying, "I went to the market," I would have to say, "I market went." And to make things even more complex, the subject usually wasn't spoken if it was clear whom we are talking about. So it was an exercise in faith to allow myself to say, "market went" and trust that people would know what I was talking about.

The challenge was to let go of the ingrained patterns in my mind. One time in the middle of class, I laughed out loud with the realization that speaking Japanese was like speaking Yoda. Studying hard, I am. Confused, I am. Tired, I am.

And so the class went, day after day of being barraged with a language that made no sense to me. After two weeks I began to lose all hope. But in the middle of the third week, something magical happened. I suddenly understood. It was not a progressive moment, but more like an instantaneous epiphany.

I was no longer watching lips move without understanding. From that moment forward, my life in Japan changed. Instead of being on the outside, I finally began to understand what was really going on. Or at least, that was what I told myself.

I arrived back in Shinjo, excited about my newfound ability to speak and understand. I no longer needed to be a passive participant, but could be more active. With this new confidence, I began to look at something else I found curious about Japanese culture: religion. I had seen shrines in people's homes, but I didn't understand their significance. I did not see what was holding this system together. I was told that the Shinto religion was a way of connecting with nature and our ancestors. But I wanted to see what that really meant.

As I had some skill in writing grants from college, I wrote a two-page paper asking for funding for research on the Japanese religion. I proposed to write three articles that would be published in the city newspaper. It took about a month for the newspaper to get back to me with confirmation.

Uematsu Sensei, my direct superior at the school, did not approve. This was when my real Japanese lessons began. Uematsu took me aside and told me he didn't think it was a good idea. I was confused. Why would learning about their religions be a problem?

Uematsu explained that it was complicated, and it would be difficult for someone who was not Japanese to understand. I agreed, then explained that was the reason I wanted to do the research to begin with. He did not insist but he suggested strongly, which in Japanese culture should have been enough for me to drop it.

After the conversation, I felt demotivated. I vented to Miyu one evening, but she smiled at me and said I did not understand something. "In Japanese society," she explained, "your direct superior is responsible for all of your actions, as if they were his own. So if you fail, it is a direct reflection on Uematsu, as if he had failed." She explained that in Japanese culture, hierarchy was essential and, with that, shared responsibility for everything. So if I were to take a risk, I would be taking it not only for myself, but also for Uematsu. And, in turn, Uematsu would be taking the risk for the school.

Another experience drove this home. In our school, each class put on a show in the auditorium. During the show, one of the classes put a big-screen TV on the stage. They turned on a pornographic movie. Through a very loud, echoing microphone, the woman in the film screamed as she was having sex. It was so shocking for me because parents and the city council members were at the event. I was sitting with my girlfriend at the time, and she started getting sexually harassed by all the young boys, asking her how she liked the film.

I was infuriated. I went to the vice principal, with whom I was quite close, and expressed my outrage. I demanded, "How can we let this happen? Who will be punished for this?"

He responded, "Andy, the teacher of that class was responsible for it. But actually, it's not the teacher's responsibility. It's my responsibility, because I'm responsible for that teacher. And actually, it's not even only my responsibility, because the principal is responsible for me, who's then responsible for this teacher. We as a school are responsible for what happened."

I was utterly stunned. I said, "The teacher knew the class was going to show the movie. He's the only one responsible."

"No, Andy," he said. "We are all responsible."

I was now beginning to understand the culture. The conformity I had witnessed for the first year was closely tied to a deep sense of responsibility to the group. Raised in the US, my worldview had been about independence. All my life I had been told that I would go to college and live my own life. It was foreign to me to put a group's wellbeing above my own. Yet this was my lesson.

Still, I was determined to move forward. With a very light touch, I told Uematsu I would study the religions of Japan and write the papers.

## CHAPTER 15
# STUDYING RELIGION —AND MYSELF

I began my journey on a bright Monday morning. I left from the Shinjo station to go to a Buddhist monastery about an hour north. I had phoned them two weeks earlier to share what I was planning and ask if it would be possible to spend a week. The person on the phone was not quite sure what I was saying, but finally relented.

I showed up at the monastery wholly unprepared. It was beautifully perched at the top of the mountain, about 200 meters above the skyline with a pagoda nestled between the trees at the top. The courtyard connecting all of the structures together was hundreds of years old and was beautiful. I felt as if I was entering an entirely new universe.

I had not been to an active monastery before, nor was I aware of the customs. I walked through one of the sliding doors and was met with complete silence. The few monks who were there swept the floors and moved around me as if I was not there. I thought maybe they believed I was a tourist who had gotten lost.

I finally caught the attention of one of the young monks and asked if he could help me. Looking confused, he left. Minutes later, the person with whom I had spoken on the phone showed up. As he looked at me, I had the sense that he was reconsidering his offer. He confirmed that I would be living like a monk for the week. He twisted his head as he spoke, which I took to mean, "I don't think so." Uematsu Sensei had twisted his head the same way when he told me he didn't think my idea was a good one.

After confirming, my monastery contact brought me to a simple room with a tatami mat floor. A bed was rolled up in the corner, and a small table sat in the middle of the room. I was told that morning prayer would begin at 5 a.m. and food would be served three times a day in this room. There was daily cleaning, but I was told that this was not required of me.

So there I sat in silence. The first day was excruciating. I was addicted to stimulus, so I wasn't accustomed to or comfortable with sitting still. And this was only my first hour!

I was brought dinner in the evening and told to be prepared for prayer in the morning. The sunrise did not feel like it could come soon enough, but eventually, in the morning I walked to the prayer hall where I was ushered into the central sanctum. The temple was broken into two sections, the inner for the monks and the outer for visitors.

Because I was there to experience the culture, I was given a front row seat. I was instructed to kneel, cross my ankles and rest my butt on the back of my legs, while keeping my back straight. I was unaccustomed to this position and I squirmed, trying to make sure that blood circulated down to my feet. A monk noticed and suggested that I sit if the pain got too great. I decided to press on and feel the full experience.

In time, the head monk arrived and I heard him say in Japanese, "What is this foreigner doing in here?"

The assistant monk answered, "The foreigner speaks Japanese."

I held back my smile as I imagined his face. He just grunted. The following day I was placed on the outside of the circle.

But for the moment I was inside, with the monks. As I sat with my eyes closed, listening to the prayers, I had a hard time thinking of anything other than my knees. By now, they were starting to feel numb and I began wondering how long it would take before I wouldn't feel them at all. To top it off, there were no walls separating the temple from the outside—just windows with nothing inside. The cold wind from the outside chilled me.

As I squirmed to get comfortable, I kept hearing something that sounded like a slap. I did not know what it was, but I heard it about every three minutes. I could hear it getting closer, almost like a lightning strike approaching. Then I felt a soft touch on my shoulder. The touch was then followed by the same smack that I had heard, but now it was against my back. I later learned that I had been smacked by a *"Keisaku,"* a wooden stick used to manage sleepiness or lapses of concentration. I jumped, but then went back to struggling to relax my legs.

I had just finished my first meditation and the only thing I felt was that it couldn't get any worse. I quietly went back to my room and waited for food and meditation. I spent the next days walking around the shrine in silence. My brain was frantically searching for something to hold on to, a thought to break down and digest. But now I had only myself and a few monks who walked quietly through the space, not wanting any contact.

It was the first time in my life that I was away from the stimulus of distraction, which had always allowed me to move away from uncomfortable thoughts. The first days were torture. I needed interaction and stimulus. I was unable to find quiet in my mind. The only thought I had was, "How many more days do I have to endure this?" My experiment to understand Japanese religion felt as if it had become an endurance test. The study became less about the Buddhist tradition and more about how I would survive a week of this.

This same routine continued for six straight days. After struggling with the tension of not being able to do anything, I finally surrendered sometime during the fourth day. The humming sound slowly dissipated and I was left with the peace that comes from calm.

Without the opportunity to fall back on distraction, I could hear my thoughts for the first time. I was no longer reacting to my thoughts. There was a person inside to whom I had never been introduced. The voice was calm and only appeared to show up when I did not react to the thoughts that continuously popped up. The peace in this voice was something I had not experienced. It was honest and loving and able to speak words that did not feel as though they came from me. It was as if they were generated from the ether, channeled from a power greater than myself. I felt an utter peace in the sadness that I carried with me for so many years. I had touched a part of myself that I did not know existed.

When I climbed down the mountain on the final day, I found it difficult to write about the experience. I had expected that I would be having long discussions and documenting all of the things I had learned. Instead, my lessons were very personal. My search to understand the Japanese religion became a journey into myself. I have to laugh as that was clearly the best way to understand the religion. But I was too occupied with achievement at the time to understand that was the lesson.

In order to understand religion in Japan, I realized I needed to first understand myself. The god I was looking to find was not outward, but inward. The voice inside my head was something that I later discovered was referred to as the "Third Eye." According to Buddhism, the Third Eye is the symbol of spiritual awakening, whereas to Westerners it symbolizes clairvoyance. I did not place any religious value on this experience. I was just shocked that something that clear lived inside of me.

My journey into the Shinto religion was a bit subtler. I was told that 80 percent of the Japanese practiced the Shinto religion. But when I asked people about it, I could hardly find anyone who identified as a practitioner. What I discovered was that the Shinto religion had become so embedded in the Japanese psyche that it was more a way of living rather than a formal, practiced religion. This was most visible in the shrines that could be found in just about every home. Pictures of faces going back as far as photography existed were attached to the ceiling and tilted downward, letting everyone know they came from something greater than themselves, that they were part of a legacy to be cherished and cared for. Incense would burn daily in front of the shrine. It was a constant reminder of their place in the world.

One of the teachers at a school I often visited was a Shinto priest. Nothing about his looks indicated he was any different than anyone else. He would tell dirty jokes and act almost boyish at times. When I would ask him about the religion, he would never answer. I began to think he did not understand the religion. But then I realized he was having trouble sharing how the religion was the underpinning of Japanese society. What I learned, and loved, was Shintoism's connection to the earth. I was reminded of the Native Americans and their harmony with the land. Although not spoken with such vigor, Shintoism was the invisible glue that made sense of so much of what I witnessed.

Out of all of the things I discovered in studying Japanese religion, the thing most challenging to grasp was sexual morality. Raised a Catholic, I was accustomed to feeling guilt for just about everything. It appeared that there were other standards in Japan. I remember one weekend outing with all of the teachers. While drinking, two of the teachers had an affair. I was shocked. Everyone knew about it, yet it was quietly ignored. There was nothing to discuss because apparently, nothing had happened. No one displayed shame or judgment. Just a night that was behind us. If I tried to discuss anything about what happened the night before, I would be met with blank stares, as if we had attended different events. The same was true for drunkenness. It reminded me of the saying, "What happens in Vegas, stays in Vegas." But in this case, it was an entire country. I had a hard time separating my ideas of morality and the Japanese acceptance that "Sometimes, shit happens."

Not unlike the Detroit factory and the sheep station before that, the Japanese had created a shared social consciousness that I was finally beginning to feel. Yes, it had its flaws, but so did each other culture I had immersed myself in. I felt incredibly lucky to see life from an entirely different perspective, from an entirely different set of values and norms.

Each time I entered into a new culture and context, I was learning more and more deeply about my own self, how I experience the world, and how many things I still had to learn. In all these adventures, I was seeking inner peace and freedom. But I didn't know that yet.

## CHAPTER 16

# IRRECONCILABLE DIFFERENCES

**E**ventually, I was able to write my articles on what I had learned about religion in Japan, and they were published in the local newspaper in Shinjo. I experienced my first taste of success and it felt addictive. I wondered what I could do next.

One evening after work I was sitting under my bed watching Japan's national sport, sumo. I was struck by an idea: Why not bring foreigners together to participate in an international sumo tournament? Teams would compete against one another while everyone learned about the sport. The idea was already complete in my head. Now I just needed to invite the universe to create it. I was Kevin Costner in *Field of Dreams*: "Build it and they will come."

Given the response to my first idea, I was worried about sharing my vision with Uematsu Sensei. But I knew I had to get his approval. I told him my idea and, true to form, he ran his fingers through his hair, shook his head, and said something I learned to dread, "Soo ka na."

In Japanese, the word for "no" is seldom, if ever, used. In its place, they usually use a phrase that means, "So, interesting." Given that Japanese culture is highly empathetic, one is simply supposed to know that this phrase means "no." It's considered rude to put someone in a position where they're forced to say no. So, a nod of the head and a "Soo ka na" should be enough for you to get a clue.

When I pushed Uematsu, he said, "Foreigners could never understand sumo."

"Why?" I asked.

"You need to be Japanese to understand sumo," he said.

I said, "Well, of course if you're Japanese, you'll have a better understanding of how it works. But you could also learn a lot just by reading and participating."

"Yes," he said, "But you can never really understand."

Yet I was stubborn enough to acknowledge his unwillingness and still push on, however softly. This time I would be under a watchful eye. Every step, Uematsu would check and double-check that I did not ignore any Japanese custom, which would have dishonored him and his work.

I made all the arrangements, including bringing in a sumo wrestler to train participants. Before going to meet the wrestler, Uematsu made certain that I had "omiagi," the traditional gift given when visiting or coming back from a vacation. I was armed with a bottle of sake so large it filled both of my arms.

Uematsu Sensei reviewed how I would introduce myself. He had no faith that I had learned the basics of Japanese living after more than a year. In the end, I relented and let him join me for the visit. In retrospect, I realize the visit would never have happened without him joining me. He had been so worried that I would offend others, and he did not want to be seen as a bad guide.

The tournament came and was a big success. Thirty participants from around Japan came to Shinjo and we held the first annual

Shinjo Sumo Tournament. The Japanese were impressed to see so many foreigners wearing "*mawashis*," the traditional belts worn by wrestlers.

This marked a pivotal moment for me in my time in Japan. Although I had spent much time learning the language and studying the culture, it was becoming more and more apparent to me that I would never be accepted as part of this society. To the Japanese, I would always be a foreigner, an outsider.

This came to a head in the closing weeks of my time in Japan. I felt a deep sense of achievement after the completion of the sumo event. I smiled at Uematsu, sharing the happiness that I felt with my success. But I was met with a blank face. I knew he was not happy that it happened. But I thought he would be relieved that it had gone well. In my heart I was hoping he would acknowledge that it was even valuable to the city and the participants. Just as I was sorely missing my father's approval, I wanted his affirmation. Yet, as with my father, I had defied his wishes, and that would always remain the point.

I asked him what he thought about the event. He was abrupt. He smiled in an uncomfortable way, only saying that foreigners would never understand sumo, that it is a sport that only Japanese can truly understand. At this point I was fuming. I'd spent over a year learning the language and studying the culture. I'd done my best to integrate, yet in the end he was right. In defying him and putting on the event regardless of his wishes, I proved that I was in fact not willing to adapt to the culture.

At the time I was so angry that I said, "You know the Nan-King massacre?" This was an infamous massacre committed by the Japanese in China that is not written about in Japanese history books. I continued, "Well, your country killed hundreds of thousands of people in China and it's not written about in your history books. Sometimes you need a foreigner to understand your own culture."

After these parting words, I spent my final weeks sitting next to Uematsu silently. He was right. I did not belong in Japan. I was not ready to compromise my wishes to cater to those of my superiors. I could not deny that I learned to love much of this culture, but at the same time it was not my culture. I realized I didn't really have a culture. I had been trying to create my own personal culture by picking parts of cultures that I liked and discarding the parts I didn't like. In some ways, Japan became a relationship with irreconcilable differences. I loved the culture, but there were just too many things that we could not work out.

Japan had one last thing to teach me before I left. This would come in the form of a special person.

## CHAPTER 17

# EXPERIENCING "ISHIN-DENSHIN"

O ne night when I was sick of watching TV, I decided to go find a bar. Shinjo didn't have many bars and they were hard to find. It was a medieval city and there were no straight streets. This was to make it harder for invaders, as they would have to turn more corners and would get confused.

As I walked through the streets, I saw a discreet sign for a bar I had not seen before. I walked down the stairs and into a room that could only fit about fifteen people comfortably. It was the basement of a house and it felt more like a bedroom that had been converted into a bar for the night.

I walked to the bar and sat down. There were the usual stares and twitters as people saw me. I ordered a beer and began to regret my experiment. Suddenly, a man behind me put a microphone in my hand and ordered me to sing a Beatles song from the karaoke machine. I rejected him, but as the song continued, everyone insisted. I realized it would be more embarrassing for me to decline than to sing. So I sang, "Let it Be."

I'm no singer, and I'm certainly no Paul McCartney. I sang off-key and strained to reach certain notes. It was humiliating. Yet in true Japanese style I was complimented as if I had performed like Pavarotti at the Met.

I was finishing my drink and preparing to leave when I noticed a man sitting two chairs away from me. His hair was dyed yellow and he had thirteen earrings on one ear. He seemed to be the type of person I would do my best to avoid.

He introduced himself as Hideki and asked me where I was from. I politely answered, hoping I could move to avoid the typical questions that I had heard so often. "Why are you here?" "What do you like about Japan?" "Do you like Japanese women?" After living a year in Japan I was beginning to think there was a handbook on how to annoy foreigners with the same questions over and over.

But he sat quietly for the most part. Then he asked me to help him translate his favorite songs. He loved Aerosmith and he could sing all of their songs, but he didn't understand a word of what he was singing. We went song by song and he laughed out loud as I translated the songs into Japanese.

I quickly discovered that Hideki was different. He didn't carry himself as the other Japanese, yet he still had a deep compassionate gaze, which was the quality I loved in the Japanese. We shared a great night of laughter and arranged to see one another again. Our friendship was immediate. With Hideki, I made one of the deepest, most fulfilling connections in my life. We wanted to spend as much time together as possible. I had about eight months left in Japan.

After spending time together for a few weeks, some problems began to emerge. As a teacher, I was supposed to lead by example. Hanging out with someone with yellow hair and ear piercings was not the example my superior had in mind. Hideki became aware of this challenge way before I did. One day when he came to visit me, to my surprise, he had dyed his hair black and removed all his earrings.

Hideki was engaged to a woman named Maki, and the three of us would spend every weekend driving to somewhere else for a field trip. As Hideki and I would enjoy being together, Maki would often laugh at us. One evening I shared the story of my mother's death with him. He started crying. I saw in his eyes the pain that I was unable to feel myself, because I had denied and escaped it for so long. My friend Miyu, and now Hideki, allowed me to see my own pain through empathy. It had been a long time since I had felt fully seen.

I was a broken man and with Hideki, I did not need to hide it. The connection was beyond words. It was one of those extremely rare moments when you see someone as they are and feel fully accepted for everything you are. Hideki was teaching me something I had forgotten: love in its purest form. Love without want or need—love for another person, just as they are.

As our time together came to a close, we would get emotional at the thought of me leaving. In the middle of discussions we would both start crying as others looked on in confusion. The week before my departure we vowed to spend as much time as we could together. He came to my apartment each night and he'd sleep in the next room. We were cherishing our last moments together.

Hideki and I have been in contact ever since. I still call him every year on his birthday, December 30. We're both always quite amazed at how well I speak Japanese twenty years later. Holding onto Japanese is holding onto my relationship with Hideki. Hideki and Maki married two years after I left. I was unable to attend, so at the wedding they left a chair vacant for me. I didn't find that out until I visited them several years later. I was looking through their wedding photos and kept noticing the vacant chair. I asked Hideki about it, and when he told me it had been for me, I burst into tears.

The connection I shared with both Miyu and Hideki is something the English language does not have a word for. But the Japanese call it *"ishin-denshin."* It literally translates as "what the mind thinks, the heart transmits." Sometimes translated into English as "telepathy" or "sympathy," *ishin-denshin* is also commonly rendered as "heart-to-heart communication."

In learning the Japanese language and culture, I observed a deep feeling of connectedness that I hadn't experienced anywhere else in my life. In the West, we tend to state things literally and explain things ad infinitum to be understood. But the Japanese don't require that to communicate even deep emotions.

If nothing else, Japan taught me that deep human connection, which transcends words, is the most beautiful and healing thing in the world. And for me, the deepest way to find that connection was through my pain. Sharing my pain and being seen in that pain opened and healed my heart like nothing I could ever have imagined. I had spent so much time trying to suppress and escape my pain, when what I really needed to do was share it.

## CHAPTER 18

# AN UPWARD AND INWARD TREK

As the time neared for me to leave Japan, I still wasn't prepared to go back to the US. I was not prepared to meet my father again. I was also scared that I would turn into one of those 9-to-5 people. In what felt like a last-ditch effort to avoid coming home, I decided to take another year to travel the world. I had saved enough money working in Japan to pay for more travels.

One evening I took out a map and placed it on the dinner table, trying to decide where I'd go this time. I had travelled the northern route, overland from Bangkok to Germany, and this time I decided to take the southern route. It seemed like a good idea, but in reality, the logistics were far more difficult. Because I was an American citizen, I would encounter a few countries along the way that were not welcoming to me.

I flew directly from Tokyo to Bangkok. By this time I knew what to expect, so the hawkers trying to pull me into their taxis was no longer new and scary. Bangkok was a home base to many travelers who used it as a jumping-off point for longer trips. The flights were cheap and the connections many.

I decided to make my way to Nepal. The flight on the dual-propeller plane was alarming: we were forced to deplane, twice. First, the right propeller wouldn't start, and next the left one wouldn't start. I was anxious, but I didn't have the confidence to say I would take the next flight. We eventually landed in Kathmandu where I was overwhelmed by the poverty I saw. There were many open sewers and people wandering the streets barefoot. Compared to the places where I had travelled before, this was something different.

In spite of this, there was a warmth in the people that was remarkable. I was often asked into people's homes for tea, where they had mud floors. I was terribly anxious that I was being pulled into a trap, only to later realize that this was always an act of generosity without any desire for money.

On one occasion I was walking in the countryside and two children came toward me, observing my every move. As I walked closer to where they lived, the mother came out and waved me to their home. Calling it a home was, to me, a bit of an overstatement. It was a mud structure in the shape of a dome. Twice she invited me in and I declined, as I thought of all the trouble I could get into. Maybe they would put a ransom on my head?

Looking into the woman's eyes, I realized I had no reason to be fearful. I entered her home and was utterly perplexed at the incredible care she gave me. She took what appeared to be a special glass from the shelf, as if she was using the best for her guest. She made me tea and we sat and mimicked conversation. Although we had no language in common, we had no difficulty communicating. I gestured and pointed with smiles and frowns to express myself, and an hour and a half later we were laughing together as if we had been friends for years.

The kids slowly built up their own confidence and touched my skin. So for me, a day of sightseeing slowly turned into a day of humility. I was shown the beauty of generosity in the midst of material scarcity. It was as if to say, we are happy with everything that we have been gifted, as opposed to fixating on the things that we do not have. I wanted to leave money, but I decided not to for fear that I might taint the purity of the experience. I saw true joy without material want. I realized that it was arrogant for me to pity people who have apparently less than I do. They often have more than we could ever imagine.

In Kathmandu, I noticed that people were traveling to Pokhara to travel up through the Himalayas. I had never spent time in the mountains and thought it would be a great opportunity to learn something new. What I didn't know was that people would often spend years to prepare for such a trip. There were guidebooks and warnings galore. Yet, quite ignorantly, I thought I could figure it out.

Getting to where we would start the hike was my first warning that this was not going to be easy. As we traveled on the road cut into the mountain, we observed that there were no safety barriers between us and the cliffs that were inches from the road's edge. The sheer cliff fell into a gorge 300 meters deep. There would be no surviving if the driver had a bad day.

I felt a mix of fear and excitement as I set off on my first mountain trek. It would be twenty-eight days altogether. In that time I would see no cars or TV's, or any of the conveniences that I had become so accustomed to seeing throughout my life. And the hikes were far more challenging than I had expected. We would wake at 5 a.m. and walk for between five and seven hours a day, often straight up and down mountains. The paths were not always well-marked, so we had to do a lot of backtracking.

Although there was no planned group, a group of us banded together—some better prepared than others. I made friends with a British professor who was very serious about the whole trek and was rather disappointed in my lack of preparation. I think he felt that if I could make it, it would invalidate the sacredness of the trip he had spent so much time planning. Yet I was happy to travel with him. He pulled out his maps and descriptions on a daily basis, and it was as if I had my own tour guide for the trip.

There were no arrangements for accommodations along the

way: whatever village we ended up in, we found a house to sleep in. Whoever we stayed with would cook for us. They provided a simple menu always containing *momos*, a dumpling that is the Tibetan favorite.

The beauty of these mountains was breathtaking. The nights we spent sitting with the people running the guest houses made it doubly special. I would often sit next to the fire as they prepared our meal. I felt as if I was traveling back in time.

What I didn't expect was that this journey would become a time for me to reflect. Away from all of my usual stimuli, my mind began to settle. I felt a connection with nature. Everything felt much simpler. Much of my traveling prior to this consisted of visiting famous landmarks. But this was about being connected with the environment—enjoying the moments around the fire and experiencing life in a whole new light.

The situation was quite similar to that of the Buddhist monastery, and the special day I experienced on the Australian ranch before that. In each of those situations, I felt a deeper sense of being, as if I was no longer the center of the picture, but rather a part of something much greater. There is a state that is often spoken about, in spiritual circles, of an elevated state of being: oneness. I began to sense this state where my identity was no longer center stage. In the grandeur of these fabulous mountains, I felt a sense of comfort that I had missed ever since my mother's death. In that moment, life and death somehow all made sense to me.

After circling the Annapurna mountain range over the course of almost a month, I came off the mountain a different man. I was in love with the beauty of life—the beauty that can only be found when you look inward. The Third Eye I had accidentally discovered in the Buddhist temple in Japan had become my travel companion. The quiet voice spoke when it wasn't being distracted with stimuli.

I saw how quickly I could get lost in the buzz of life: a TV in the corner of the room. A taxi driver yelling at someone who had just cut him off. An offhand remark that hid an unspoken distrust. I was not able to find peace in places that were full of distraction. I wanted to be more open and present to the voice, yet I was finding it challenging. I had discovered how to be Buddha on the mountain. Now, my challenge was to bring that deep awareness back into the stimulus of the city, to find that same peace within myself without hiding away in a mountain.

## CHAPTER 19

# DISINHERITED

After coming off the mountain, I was planning to start the overland crossing from Nepal all the way to Europe. As I mapped out the journey, I met people coming for the next stop, India. As we all sat around a table at a pub in Nepal, each of the travelers went into great detail describing the ailments they suffered during their trip. They argued about who lost more weight from their sicknesses.

Listening to all this misery made the thought of traveling through India alone completely unappealing. I loved the challenge of getting through a foreign land, but the prospect of fighting disease brought me no excitement. Although I didn't usually like guided tours, I thought I might make an exception for India. And after arriving, I was happy I did.

I had never felt such an assault on my senses. After the peace of the Annapurna mountains, the madness of India was that much greater. I received no respite from the constant abrasive sounds, smells, and sights. People with disabilities would force themselves upon me looking for money. One time, a man whose arm was not attached to its bone was raising his limp arm for money. It was all overwhelming. The tour operator did his best to lead us to less trafficked areas, but it was a discount tour so we camped and cooked for ourselves, and we didn't have a lot of time to rest. Wherever we landed, we stayed busy putting up tents and cooking dinner.

The six-week tour took me throughout the entire country. We made our way from Varanasi to Kanyakumari, the southernmost point of India. The landscape flew by from back of the open-air truck we rode in. Early on my trip, I was on a small boat in the Ganges, India's holiest river. Hundreds of people are cremated every day along its banks to liberate their souls to find nirvana and be reborn. It is believed that anyone who dies in Varanasi breaks the cycle of death and rebirth and achieves nirvana (*moksha*). For those who cannot afford to cremate their loved one, the alternative is to wrap the body in cloth and drop it into the water.

As we were floating along the banks, I saw a small white cloth in the water. At first glance, I assumed it was litter. As I looked closer, I saw that it was the wrapped body of a baby. My heart sank. I was looking at a child who would never have a chance to grow into maturity. I sat with the guilt. With the money I was spending on this trip, I could have possibly saved this child's life. I felt a deep sense of discomfort, as if I was now a spectator to this misery. I could feel myself shutting down emotionally, something I was familiar with. I wanted to break down in tears, but I couldn't. I was confronted with more than I could handle. The only way I could survive was by strengthening the barrier between my head and my heart.

The excitement of this trip came less from the traveling and more from the company. Along the way, I was attracted to a young Swiss girl who was traveling with two friends. She was reserved in her expression, like just about all Swiss people

I have known. But I found her quiet way to be mysterious and intriguing. I stared at her during the trip, hoping to sit opposite her so I could always keep my eye on her. Her friends began to notice my obvious gaze, and they began to warn her to be careful of the American.

Eventually we spoke, and I learned her name was Irene. She wasn't looking for a fling, and her friends were quick to judge any contact between us. It was uncomfortable because we had to act as if we were not too interested in one another to avoid creating tension between her and her friends. I saw that her friends were very concerned about being seen as impulsive. Over the six-week tour, it became obvious that we had become more than just friends. But Irene didn't want our relationship to be made public.

By the time we reached our final destination, I had gotten sick twice, despite my best efforts to watch what I ate and drank. I was now excited to spend time with Irene. She left her friends and we continued onward together. We went through Egypt, Israel, Jordan, and Syria, loving everything in our path. Irene hadn't planned on traveling as long as I had, so I decided to cut my trip short and spend the last few months of my year traveling in Switzerland.

But before transitioning to Switzerland, I went back to the US for what I thought would be a short visit to coordinate things. It would turn out to be a pivotal moment in my life. Returning home after so many years of coming and going was continuing to create great tension between me and my father. He would repeat, over and over again, that I needed to "start" my life.

Three days after I arrived home, my father came home in a manic state. Although it made me very uncomfortable, I had grown accustomed to it over the years. He began by telling me how backwards Europe was. At one point he exclaimed, "They don't even have air-conditioned movie theaters!"

I was quick to defend myself, trying to reason with him that this was only a replacement of my original plan and I would see how it went. He was unrelenting. He yelled at me, the same way I remember him yelling at my mother when I was little. He yelled at the top of his lungs with such a rage that I was fearful he would begin hitting me. He told me that if I chose to go back to Switzerland, I would be dead to him. I would inherit nothing and our relationship would be over.

I tried to slow down and explain, but each word just enraged him more. He would not let the conversation continue until I guaranteed him that I would not return to Switzerland. I would not make that guarantee, and that sent him into a full-blown rage.

He came running toward me and shouted, "You have thirty minutes to get yourself and everything you own out of my house. Whatever is left will be thrown away." As I sobbed and began packing, he continued, "You are dead to me! You are written out of my will and I never want to have contact with you again." He kept repeating, "You are dead to me! You are dead to me!"

I was at a complete loss. Although being with him never felt like home, at least I had had a place to go back to. I was now truly on my own. I had no safety blanket to fall into if something went wrong. I quickly grabbed the things I could and left the things that were too difficult to move. It was as if I had experienced a fire and everything I associated with my past was now gone.

I ran out of the house and found temporary sanctuary with my friend, Ted, who helped me come to grips with my new reality. The next day, my father called me to confirm that he would, indeed, write me out of his will. I called my brothers and asked them to stand with me and tell my father that his behavior was not acceptable. I wanted us to tell him together that we would not accept that any member of our family would be banished for living the life they wanted to live. But they wanted nothing to do with it. I felt as if I was not being accepted for who I was by my family. I was alone in the world. When no one came to give me the support I sorely needed, I realized my life was my own. I would need to search out my own new family. I would need to make my own way in the world.

Then something magical happened. It felt like a scene out of a movie. After waking up on the sofa at Ted's house, I walked to the bathroom, looked in the mirror and thought, "This is the moment you've been waiting for. What do you stand for? What do you stand against?" I knew that if I stayed in the US, I would never be able to look at myself and respect the reflection I saw. I decided, without question, to return to Switzerland and leave the promise of some future wealth behind.

Up until that moment I was largely unaware of the stranglehold my father had had on me. Even when I was not in contact with him, the mere thought that he could show up at any time was incapacitating. It would often take me months to recover from the insecurity that arose in me from our talks. Yet now, by his own will, I was set free. He anticipated that by threatening to disinherit me, he could force me to stay. But instead, it reinforced the necessity for me to leave.

Strangely, this did not bring me anxiety, but rather a deeper sense of determination to succeed. Instead of going to Switzerland just to see how it would go, I went with the solid determination to make it succeed. From this moment forward, I would succeed or fail on my own merit. This was liberation.

In retrospect, this was the greatest gift my father ever gave me. In spite of my conscious decisions that went against his wishes, in the back of my mind I always had thoughts like, *Will he approve or disapprove? How will he react when I tell him?* Now, I would be accountable to no one but myself. It was both scary and exciting. I was the baby bird that was just pushed out of the nest, and it was time to fly on my own.

# CHAPTER 20
# SWISS COLD TO VIENNESE OPPORTUNITY

I landed in Switzerland, thinking it would be easy. Little did I know. Irene lived in a small town called Thun, a quaint village surrounded by beautiful mountains. The surroundings are so idyllic that it's hard not to fall in love with the storybook quality.

What I was wholly unprepared for was the people. The Swiss are mountain people, which gives them a certain emotional restraint. Switzerland was the antithesis of Japan. The Japanese had a silent communicative social awareness. The Swiss, in contrast, were also silent, but in a cold and strangely emotionless way. I felt very isolated there.

Irene and I had a lot of talks about me staying there, and I told her, "I just can't find comfort here. I feel like I'm living in an outdoor prison." She would try to get me to go out and socialize, which I did. But even then I noticed that people just weren't particularly open or free-spirited. It felt very controlled. No one showed any vulnerability or shared sense of being in the world, as I had experienced in Japan.

Irene's mother was utterly confused by my background. She asked, "What did you study?"

I would reply that I did a general study that taught me how to think. She looked at me with eyes of disgust, undoubtedly thinking, *How could my daughter end up with someone who had no trade?* We spent hours discussing how someone could graduate from college with no specific trade. She would ask over and over again, "Yes, I understand you graduated. But what does that allow you to do?"

I learned quickly that to gain employment in Switzerland you needed a trade. A person could not simply declare themselves a photographer, for example. They first needed to finish their studies, and even that was not enough. They would then need to apprentice with someone in the field. In essence, I was helpless to find a job because no one would hire me without the proper credentials. And given that I was not even sure what I wanted to do, it was not going to be easy.

Instead of wasting time finding work, I decided to join intensive German classes, which was the primary language in Switzerland. I figured if anyone was going to hire me, German language skills would be required. I went to the nearest city which was the capital, Bern. I spent the next three months in extensive German courses, learning grammar and pronunciation. The irony of this class was that the Swiss did in fact not speak German but rather Swiss German, a dialect. To my ears, it sounded like singing the language instead of speaking it.

Every day after leaving class, I would try to speak to people. I would be met with blank stares. I felt as if I had invested all of this time and had nothing to show for it. One day, I stood at the train counter trying to order a ticket to Thun. I repeated the city name over and over again, in disbelief that the woman could not understand my words. Then, in one last-ditch effort, I sang the word, and I exaggerated, as if trying to provoke her. I said, "Thuuuuuunnnn," drawing it out for extra theatrics. Then the woman smiled, relieved that she finally understood me. I was ready to pack my bags.

I had made a friend from my trip on the Trans-Siberian railway whose mother had a living space available in Vienna. I told Irene I could not last in Switzerland. Between the strict employment policies and the even stricter emotionlessness that I was experiencing, I was not going to make it another month. We decided to try our luck somewhere else where we were both foreigners: Vienna, the adopted home of Mozart.

Vienna was a dream. Irene and I lived right behind the city hall, and the city was full of wonderful surprises. Most importantly, they understood my German! I was amazed by all the buildings with their history of artists, musicians, and philosophers. But with money still a concern, I had little time to waste.

I went to the American Chamber of Commerce, believing that if I contacted all the US companies based in Vienna, I would surely find a job. I ended up writing to over 100 companies and sending personalized letters that included my curriculum vitae. I waited and waited. It took about a month for me to receive the one and only response, which came from Proctor and Gamble. They were looking to fill a product management position. I drove forty-five minutes to the interview, feeling a bit depressed from the many rejections I had already received.

My fate was sealed during the interview when I shared that I had been rejected by so many other potential employers. My eyes were full of emotion as I shared my plight. I was hoping that the interviewer would take pity on me and offer me the job. But I would have no such luck. She politely escorted me to the door and offered me a jar of pre-mixed peanut butter and jelly in a jar.

I was devastated. I thought my sheer determination would be enough, but it wasn't proving so. In my desperate state, I started getting creative. Now that I was no longer limiting my possibilities to US companies based in Austria, I could simply open the newspaper and see what was available.

One day I came across an ad for a company with a strange name, TOPCALL. It read, "International Presenter Wanted." I remember my friends speculating on everything the company could be, from call center to brothel. I learned that it was an information technologies (IT) company. Although I didn't have any specific experience in this area, I went to the interview with an open mind. I cut my hair, which had been still long from the trip, and bought a suit.

I also hoped I could upgrade the position into something more appealing. The idea of "marketing" was attractive to me, although I didn't really know what it entailed. I associated advertising with creativity, which I always found interesting. The interviewer was a man who was larger than life, Fred Zimmer, who was the company's marketing director. He walked into the room as if he was a movie director setting up a scene. His first words were, "Why do you think you can do this job?"

I shared that I had done some magic and I was accustomed to performing in front of crowds. He nodded in a way that a doctor might nod, as the patient reads out their symptoms. I went on to share that although I was interested in presenting, I would love the opportunity to grow into a marketing position.

Fred responded that no such positions were available. I went away from the interview, not really knowing how it went, nor feeling any sense of anxiety. I had resigned myself to letting things fall into place instead of forcing them, which hadn't gotten me far. Yet.

Less than a week later, I received a call from Fred with the good news. He said that not only was he going to offer me the presenter position, but just the day before, his assistant had quit and the position of assistant marketing manager was now open. He asked me if I wanted it.

Trying to stifle my excitement, I said I'd love the opportunity. He told me I would start the following week.

This part of my journey taught me an incredible lesson. I saw that the more fearful I was, the less likely I was to be open to possibilities. As I was slaving away, sending out those 100 CVs in fear and desperation, I lost perspective. I was trying to define my future in the only way I knew how: through sheer determination. I was driven to prove to my father that I could do it, and in doing so, I lost the freedom to see what was right in front of me. My job opportunity appeared as I freed myself from the need to find a job. Just like all the other opportunities that had presented themselves to me throughout the years, I was learning the same lesson over and over again. If you surrender to life, it will show you the way.

I was now twenty-six years old, living in a country I had only been in for a month. I could barely speak the language. I had only minor experience in business, and certainly nothing in marketing. Yet I was now the assistant marketing manager. I laughed because all I did was be bold enough to ask, "Do you have a marketing position?" I would spend the next years discovering exactly where that simple question would take me.

## CHAPTER 21
# RISING HIGH AND FEELING LOW

**H**ere I was in the IT business, which I knew virtually nothing about. It was 1996 and the IT bubble was starting to inflate. The company was scheduled to go public in three months on the EASDAQ, the European version of the NASDAQ. In those three months, I had to create a tour highlighting IT that I, so far, knew nothing about. This "tour" had to be presented in front of a select group of IT Directors, who were slated to hear me speak for three hours. All I can say is, be careful what you wish for.

I spent the next three months learning, and learning fast. I felt constantly behind and severely unqualified. By all standards, my manager, Fred, was a tyrant. He would constantly raise his voice in frustration and demean everyone around him. I was often called "stupid" and "incompetent." It got so bad that one day I asked him, "Why did you even hire me?"

He answered, "Because you speak English and do magic."

I replied, "You are either a genius or an idiot." He turned away without responding.

What I learned in those first few months was how to adapt. If I didn't know something, I quickly learned how to figure it out. I would often stay in the office until 10 p.m. to finish my work.

At one point I was told I needed to write the initial public offering (IPO) document for the company. I had no idea what the purpose of such a document was, or how to create it. So I sent emails to anyone whom I thought might be able to send me examples. I ended up taking the best parts of the different documents and creating something resembling a first-rate IPO offer. What this trial by fire taught me was that I could achieve just about anything I set my mind to, as long as I believed it was possible from the start.

Not long afterward, the CEO, Martin Hannah, called me into his office and had a request. Martin was a chain-smoking, heavy-drinking, loud and unapologetic man. He drank so much that on one occasion, he forgot where he parked his car. A month afterward, the hotel had called him and asked him if he was going to pick it up.

Martin told me he needed me to write two press releases a month.

My initial thought was that this was impossible. Then it dawned on me that I had already written an IPO document. How hard would it be to learn to write press releases? Instead of agreeing to his request, I came back with a request of my own. I told him that I had never written a press release and that I would need permission to fail. I knew I could certainly try, but I could not be sure I would succeed in the process.

A bit bewildered, he said, "Yes, of course, it's okay if you fail."

I left his office in high spirits. I had just been given the opportunity to learn an entirely new set of skills, and get paid while doing it. I thought to myself, "How many people pay to learn how to do this? And I'm getting paid to learn." It was a dream come true and I took advantage of every moment.

Not too long into my employment, my manager, Fred, took me aside and told me he would be quitting his job because he could no longer manage his relationship with Martin, the CEO. And so it was that I went from a long-haired hippie in India to marketing director of a multinational, publicly-listed company. I was unable to manage my own checkbook but I was now tasked with the management of a multimillion-dollar budget. With this responsibility came a lot of fear. But as all the bridges behind me had been burned, I could only move forward.

Before this moment, I had been accustomed to step away from difficult situations and miss out on the opportunity to grow—all because of my fear of failing. I could see the connection between my fear of failing and the anxiety of being chastised by my father. I saw that I was programmed to avoid pain and conflict. Now I was beginning to heal by having more compassion for myself. I no longer needed to be perfect. I just had to trust that I would be open to making sure to fail often, and fail while continuously moving forward. Before this position, I judged failure as negative. Now I celebrated it!

I felt a deep sense of accomplishment in this position. I had proven wrong all those who had doubted me. I took on the personality of a marketing director, with all of the bravado. In fact, I was still fighting for the approval of my father.

It got so bad that one day Martin called me into his office and said that my phone bill, coming in at over 1,500€, was too high.

Without blinking an eye I responded, "If it is less than this, call me back into your office because I'm not doing my job."

In my cockiness, I began to lose touch with the curiosity that had made my life so beautiful. I replaced it with money and status. And over time, I started noticing an emptiness in myself. I was utterly fearful of being alone. I would schedule activities on every night of the week so I wouldn't have to be alone with my thoughts. Irene and I were sharing space, but we were no longer emotionally connected. I was on the phone constantly, filling up all gaps in time with noise—anything to stay away from the nagging sound in my head that told me something was wrong.

Although I didn't think about it much, my childhood pain was still stuck deep inside me, and it was still driving my behavior.

It came to the surface one day at work. I finished my morning workout and headed to the office. As I walked through the door, my assistant, with whom I had worked for several years, followed me to my office. Looking anxious, she said, "Your father called several times today." She was aware that he and I were not in contact, so I believe she was expecting something bad.

I felt confused. It had been almost a decade since he had thrown me out of his house. I still wasn't over it. When he called again, all of my childhood anxiety and insecurities, which I had all but forgotten, resurfaced. I still felt like the ten-year-old boy who had just been thrown out of the house and told to walk to my mother's house in the dark. I told my assistant to forward all future calls to voicemail. I had no interest in speaking with him. I could not afford the emotional impact he made in my life.

She looked at me strangely. "Are you sure?" she asked.

"Yes," I replied, leaving no space for discussion or vulnerability. I just needed to push it aside as quickly as possible in hopes of not risking my already tightly-strung emotional state.

Soon afterward, I rang my brother to better understand what was going on. Apparently, my father had admitted himself into the psychiatric ward at the UCLA Medical Center for fear of what he might do to himself. When I heard this, a deep sense of dread overcame me. How would I feel if he were to die and I lost my last opportunity to speak with him? Would I feel as if I had lost the one shot to finally meet the father I had always wanted?

Then reality set in: I was simply incapable. My father had the power to undermine the confidence that had taken me so long to find. It felt irresponsible to risk it. I didn't feel comfortable with any scenario. I remained true to my original decision to not allow contact. But this time, I grieved. It was now my decision, not his.

I saw that the tables had turned and it was *me* giving *him* thirty minutes to get out of *my* house. Except in this case, my house was my brain. He eventually sent me a letter sharing his sadness and doing his best to justify his actions. I knew I couldn't trust him because he could turn into someone else at the drop of a hat. Although I had made the decision to reject the contact, I felt terrible inside.

I replied to his letter with one of my own, in which I included the common Serenity Prayer, which he had displayed prominently in the house as his sons were growing up. He would repeat it regularly.

*God, grant me the serenity*
*to accept the things I cannot change,*
*courage to change the things I can,*
*and wisdom to know the difference.*

I felt as if it might be the last letter I would ever send him. I did not feel any of the serenity in the prayer. I knew I couldn't change my father, and I wasn't ready to love him as he was. At least not yet.

## CHAPTER 22
# A HOLE IN MY SOUL

**M**y emotional aloofness and inner emptiness led to a separation between me and Irene. We became less like soulmates and more like roommates. Weeks would go by and we would not have sex. I would often get out of bed and pull out a VHS video of porn just to feel some sense of excitement. She eventually found the porn, and took it as a betrayal of our relationship. We drifted apart until we finally decided to separate. We had been together for five years.

I moved out and began to develop a life alone. I had not lived alone since my time in Japan and it was new. I had not known Vienna as a single male. Web dating was in its infancy and I began to publish profiles, fishing for a new relationship. Dating became a new addiction to fill the time. My brain needed it to feel some sense of peace. It was clearly not peace, but I did just about everything possible to avoid the anxiety around silence.

To satisfy my need for excitement, I would take trips to exotic locations or visit adult clubs. I plugged my calendar with so many activities that I had no time to feel alone: early morning gym, followed by work, followed by dinner and a list of weekly planned engagements. I'd often set dates in the future just to have something to look forward to—something, *anything* to keep life interesting, to create the feeling of progress. I had plenty of distractions but little to make life meaningful.

The more I tried to fill the hole in my soul, the bigger that hole got. Yes, I was getting paid a lot, but at what real cost? I was empty inside. My body would occasionally show signs of what I was feeling inside. About the only time I could stop my regular workout was when I was sick. It was as if my body was telling me, "If you are not going to take responsibility, then I will."

One night I went with a friend to a famous brothel called Babylon in the first district of Vienna. It was well known as the expensive place with the most beautiful women. The cover charge was 100€, just to walk in. As we entered the house, my heart was beating a mile a minute as I felt intense feelings of anxiety come over me.

I was raised Catholic, and from a very young age I was taught how sex was a sacred act. The sin of the flesh was forbidden. I remember back to my first girlfriend when I was scared to kiss her for fear of contracting a disease. The school I attended was very good at creating fear. Walking into this club was pulling at all of my childhood anxieties. I saw immediately what addiction must feel like. I felt the rush that comes from pushing things to the edge of the unexplored, a place where you don't know what will happen.

I sat at the bar with my friend, who was equally nervous, and we tried to gather ourselves. Occasionally, a woman would approach us and we would say, "No, thank you," as if a waiter had just asked us if we'd like our water refilled. My friend eventually found a woman to go with, and I sat there looking down at my drink. The tension was building, like the moment before you jump into cold water, dipping your feet in the water to get used to the cold.

Then I saw an attractive woman walk in. I found her attractive because of her disinterest. She did little to call attention to herself as she walked to her seat. I finally decided that if I didn't act now, I would never do it. So I walked over to the woman and asked her if she would like to join me. There was no discussion about money, as the club had strict policies and payment had been explained when we walked in the door.

She escorted me back to a room. The décor was just as you would expect in a brothel. The curtains, wallpaper, and carpet formed layer upon layer of red, as if you were looking at an impressionist painting. She gave me no instructions, so I undressed as she did the same. My heart was pumping louder and louder by the second, as I was doing the unthinkable. I was breaking every rule and I felt something freeing in overcoming all of these suppressed sexual emotions.

There were clear rules: a condom was required, there would be no kissing, and we had an hour. I began slowly. I just touched and enjoyed the company of another. I was not sure what to expect but I was hoping for intimacy. A feeling of connection. Things became more physical, as she had a routine and I was the newcomer.

When it was all finished, I felt great. I imagine it was how a crack addict feels after their first high. I had done it. I had overcome my fear and anxiety to do something I would have never imagined.

When I awoke the next morning, the high had long since disappeared. In its place came a loneliness that felt somewhere between helplessness and shame. All the judgment of good and bad slowly entered my consciousness and I felt sick. I was also fearful that someone might find out I had been to a brothel, and that I would no longer be respected. I didn't want to be seen as one of "those" types of men.

I saw that some things may feel exhilarating in the moment, but they ultimately leave you feeling empty. The closest thing I could associate this emptiness with was the loss of my mother. I felt again that familiar despair and had nowhere to turn. I was looking for something, but I had no idea what it was.

I saw how shame debilitated me. I judged myself, and in doing so, started an endless loop of self-criticism that now ran through my mind. I felt a noise in my head and I crammed my schedule with more activities to block it out.

The shame, sadness and emptiness continued for the next few weeks. Then, a single event pushed my feelings over the edge into full-blown panic. On September 11, 2001, I was in Sydney, Australia for business, eating steaks at Morton's with a group of business colleagues. Suddenly a woman rushed into the room shouting, "America is under attack. You need to find a TV."

We left our food and jumped in the first taxi we could find. When I arrived at my hotel, I turned on the TV and witnessed the event in horror. I was disturbed on an indescribably deep level. I felt the obvious empathy and grieving for the suffering of others. But on a more personal level, I couldn't stand the pain I was confronted with because it completely demolished the sense of control I had fought so hard to create in myself.

From the moment my father threw me out of the house, I had felt alone in life. In that moment, my free-spirited life had changed: I had to think about supporting myself; I was now responsible for my own life and that meant taking action. A part of my being, which had not been active until then, kicked in. That part of me had been guided by fear, the need to prove myself, and the desire for control.

Now, I had spent the previous eight years fighting for that control, to understand how things work, to feel as confident as I believed others to be. Yet in the face of this incomprehensible tragedy, I lost all control in a moment. It was as if my life was a forest that had been in drought for several years, and 9/11 was the spark that set it ablaze. I saw the possibility of nuclear Armageddon and thought, *Whom would I spend my last hours with?* In a conversation with my dear friend Warren, I asked him if I could stay with his family if there should be a nuclear war. Surprised by my overwhelming anxiety, he gave me a hug and assured me that we would continue as a civilization.

Warren was a Jewish-American whose grandparents had been killed in Auschwitz. As a child, he moved with his parents to New York to avoid the Nazis, but his grandparents remained in Europe to take care of their businesses, unaware of the impending doom. Now back in Europe, Warren now viewed life with a healthy skepticism. His mother always had a suitcase packed and ready to leave Austria at a moment's notice.

A mutual friend, who saw I could use some guidance, had introduced us to one another. Warren was happy to take me under his wing. We would meet at least three times a week and we would speak at least once a day, usually twice. He, his wife, and his daughter filled the gap of family I was sorely missing. Warren became another father figure in my life.

As I sat with the horror of the 9/11 terrorist attacks, the depression I had suppressed for years bubbled up to the surface. I looked at my life and saw no meaning, no purpose. Seeing the contrast with happy people underscored my suffering. I was overwhelmed and lost. All my normal coping mechanisms were no longer working.

I began to do a lot of soul searching. How did I get here? One day I gazed into the mirror and could not recognize the man staring back at me. I was so different from the person I saw in the mirror after my father threw me out of his house. I had become exactly the person I had never wanted to be: disconnected, focused on success, lacking curiosity, always believing I knew better than anyone else. I felt deep shame. I had lost the joy I had felt when I'd begun my job, and I was beginning to lose myself in the identity of "Director."

Now I had a dilemma. Life was comfortable. I was paid well and I made my own calendar. My salary allowed me to have my phone, my car, my vacations. How could I do better? What would I risk in leaving my job? I was wearing golden handcuffs. I knew I was not happy but I did not believe I could find anything that would satisfy me more. I told myself, "The same problems exist everywhere. Why leave when you've got this system figured out?"

I had been in my position for eight years. I had achieved quite a lot and gained a lot of credibility, but now I was bored. I had accomplished everything I had set my sights on, and had lost the passion I began with. I began to complain about everything. I did my best to ignore the voice in my head telling me to leave. I was living the dream life, but it was my nightmare. On the outside, my life appeared to be ideal. But inside, I was empty. I was lonely and disconnected from myself, but afraid to risk giving up my comfort for something unknown. The irony was that I had no comfort, just familiarity.

This was one of those challenging moments when I fell back on the words of Einstein: "We cannot solve our problems with the same thinking we used when we created them." I was stuck somewhere between knowing I was totally unhappy and needing to have assurances that whatever new job I might find would make it better. My flawed assumption was that a new job was going to solve this. I spent the next few years looking for other business opportunities. Each job interview was a reminder that my issues were not about the job. What I was longing for could not be solved with the same thinking that had gotten me here.

I was so skeptical of anyone who promised happiness that I didn't know where to begin. I saw programs promising everything from business success to eternal salvation. I sensed that anyone busy convincing me of their happiness must be hiding something themselves. I sat with this skepticism for years, and remained in a state of limbo.

It was in this skeptical, yet searching state that I met the man who would change my life forever. True to my previous life experience, he appeared just as I had given up. It was time to stop trying to solve the problem and begin following my heart again.

## CHAPTER 23

# SEEING THE TRUTH

**M**y role in my company had evolved through the years to include personal development programs for the company. Although I usually hired new trainers, someone else in the company hired a new employee. The new person's name was Cees de Bruin (pronounced "case"). He was a wide-eyed Dutchman with a contagious enthusiasm.

I was asked to join the training conducted by Cees. Although I was already scheduled with meetings, I sat in on the session and I felt a buzz in the air. I knew from the moment I entered that there was something fundamentally different in how he was approaching the training. I saw that each trainee was becoming aware of how he or she was responsible for his or her own personal growth. No one was allowed to let excuses dictate his or her choices and behavior. The training I was accustomed to was turned on its head. Instead of telling people what they "should" know, they were asked where they were holding themselves back.

Cees asked us to use our own experience as the measuring stick for our understanding of the world. This, as opposed to trusting him or whatever anyone else had to say. This might appear to be obvious, but if you dig deeper, you will find, as I had discovered on my travels, that our thinking is always viewed through the prism of past experience, the ideas of others, prejudices, opinions, and beliefs. So it was quite revolutionary for me to take my own experience seriously and trust it over whatever anyone had to tell me.

I no longer accepted people's opinions, beliefs, stories, or theories as truth. I listened to and trusted myself. I asked myself where my experience overlapped with their views, if at all. Whenever I encountered ideas or beliefs that conflicted with my own, I simply became curious. I began to ask questions. My intention was never to falsify others' claims, but rather sit with the wonder of what I could not yet understand. The consequence was an increasing confidence in what I knew from my own experience. My understanding of the world, and my ability to navigate it, was no longer based on the thoughts of others, but rather on my own.

In the class, Cees asked me, "What would you do in a sales situation if the prospect were to tell you they don't have budget?"

I thought for a moment and said, "I would accept it. It would be aggressive to insist on something they did not have any influence over."

He laughed and said, "That would be one way you could deal with it." Then he asked, "How could you take them and yourself into account? How could you stay in a relationship and still leave the possibility open?"

I thought for a good while until I eventually saw where Cees was pointing. I was assuming that there wasn't an opportunity and thereby shutting down any chance to proceed. If I remained open, then I would simply ask, "Under what conditions would there be the possibility to create a budget?" Or "How can we make sure there is a budget for this in the future?" What I learned is that my assumptions of what was and was not possible were confining me. This experience changed me forever. It was my experience. It was not explained to me in theory, but I experienced it for myself. I trusted this new experience and use it to this day.

Cees was exceptional at helping people take responsibility that they normally would have avoided. With laser precision, he would quickly pinpoint the areas where people used blame to avoid taking action. He blew apart common excuses like, "It wouldn't work anyway," or "I already tried that."

I quickly saw that, up until now, I had approached training in a profoundly limiting way. I had been telling people what they should do and how to do it, instead of empowering them to define for themselves what needed to be done. This approach took some getting used to, as it forced new awareness. I could not control the development of others as I had unsuccessfully tried for so many years. I could only give them the awareness of the responsibility they could take, and ask if they were interested in making the effort.

The major lesson for me was that if I wanted to change something in the organization, I needed to begin with myself. And after years of avoidance, I had a pile of unresolved issues to dig through. With this newfound insight and focus, I began to feel the same fire I had felt in the first few months of working in the company. I was treading new ground and I was completely uncertain of how it would work out. What I knew for certain is that something had to change, and that I would no longer accept my own avoidance.

One of my first acts was to invite my office nemesis, Gerhard, for a meeting. Throughout the years I had grown a deep hatred for him. I saw him as the type of person who would say one thing to your face and another as soon as you turned your back. I had a great distrust of him and I had quietly let it simmer for years.

Inviting Gerhard to my office to discuss this was one of the most frightening things I could do. I did not sleep the night before and I was sweating all the way up to our talk. He walked into my office and sat down. I said, "Gerhard, I would like to be honest with you. I don't trust you."

His eyes got big. He was surprised and saddened to hear it. With no defense or guardedness, he asked, "What do you see in me that makes you not trust me?" I was shocked that he didn't take it personally. He didn't make counter accusations or place blame. I suddenly felt as if I may have been the one missing something.

I went on to tell him everything I saw in him. He listened quietly. He was hurt by the conversation, but he did not defend himself. As it turned out, we began to see and trust one another. After this talk we were open to one another, even to the point that we would have lunch together and laugh at the past. When others would complain to me about him, I no longer participated and only asked them to take responsibility with him, as I had done.

What I learned in this simple interaction would change my life forever. I saw that I defined my relationship with Gerhard by how I interacted with him. But it was not he who was untrustworthy, it was me. I had not been honest with him, so how could I expect him to reciprocate?

I became aware of something quite profound, and at the same time, unnerving. I could no longer be certain if people I was interacting with were a "certain way," or if they were only that way *with me*. I could no longer discount anyone. If I had negative interactions with people, I couldn't just assume it was their problem. I had to question whether I was doing something that was triggering them. Furthermore, I had to take that into account when I projected negativity onto people. By doing so, I could learn from them things about myself of which I was unaware.

Taking responsibility for my interactions gave me a new sense of freedom I had never felt before. I used this opportunity to clear out all the skeletons in my mental closet. I called all the women I had dated, all the way back to college, to apologize. I was not exactly sure what I was sorry for, but I knew I had suppressed a lot of anger, and it came out when I felt most helpless. One by one, each of them told me of their fear of that part of me that I had kept hidden and defended, and how they dealt with it.

With Cees's guidance and support, I opened up every ugly part of my past. Nothing was out of bounds. Of course, the big issue was my relationship with my father. Ever since he had thrown me out of the house, I had carried a deep resentment towards him. I truly hated him.

One night, I was talking with Cees and he asked me about it. I told him my whole story from start to finish. As I spoke, I began to hear my own words for a change. I saw that I hadn't been in contact with the situation at this moment. Rather, I was reliving the same old memory, over and over again.

Cees asked me, "Why would your father kick you out of the house?"

I answered, "Because he was scared."

He prodded, "Why was he scared?"

I dug deep and pondered hard on that. Suddenly, the realization hit me like a ton of bricks. I said, "Because he loves me." The words came out with a deep release and I began to cry. I realized I had never grasped my father's intentions. Instead, I saw only his actions, however misguided and painful. With that release, I immediately lost all anger toward my father. I felt a deep sense of gratitude that he had dealt with his love in the only way he could. I was amazed that it had taken me so long to see the obvious.

The next day, I called my father on the telephone. He was surprised to hear my voice and the call began a bit awkwardly. I told him of my discovery. I apologized to my father for not being able to recognize his love all of those years. I cried as I spoke. I'm certain he had never received an apology from someone he had yelled at (and that was a long list). He was very appreciative. I believe this was the first time he had ever felt fully understood, without judgment.

Our relationship shifted immediately and we quickly became close. All the triggers that had previously set me off were gone. Now, instead of arguing, our calls brought us closer.

I had two occasions to see my father before his death, some two years after our reconciliation. I cherish this time with him. If I had not been given the chance to reconcile, I never would have realized that I was the co-creator in all my failing relationships. I would have lived with the idea that my father was "difficult," and left it at that. I would never have seen that I, too, had a part in the dysfunction.

I began to see that everyone I had a problem with was reacting to me. I began to wonder, *What am I doing to trigger such a response?* I no longer blamed people for what I saw, but rather, saw them as a response to the way I was engaging them. If I met someone with love, there was a greater likelihood that I would be greeted with the same love. If I met them with fear and anxiety, then I could expect the same in return. I was learning to replace hatred with love, and it was becoming addicting.

For the first time in my life, I stopped telling people what they should do and instead, I led by example. Or, as Gandhi put it so succinctly, "Be the change you want to see in the world."

## CHAPTER 24

# WHO ARE YOU?

To understand Cees, you must understand his background. Cees was a second child of divorced parents. His father was a highly opinionated authoritarian figure who would spend hours telling people all the reasons why he was right and they were wrong. In contrast, Cees' mother was frail and fearful. She used alcohol to numb her pain and anxiety. Cees was stuck in the middle of this dichotomy and did his best to balance the contrary energies.

Since his father was a businessman who relocated his family often, Cees grew up roaming the Dutch countryside and changing schools every few years. He was a nomad and had a hard time building long-term friendships. This made him very independent. He learned how to grow intellectually in order to stave off bullies. He was small in size but large in his capacity to defend himself.

In 1997, Cees was diagnosed with Non-Hodgkin lymphoma, a cancer of the glands. As he was prone to do, he took drastic action and sold everything he owned, purchased a camper van, and moved to a nudist colony. He said, "When I die, I don't want to leave anything behind."

This period of his life was remarkable because, unexpectedly, he'd felt a deep sense of peace. He told me, "The moment I accepted I was going to die, a euphoria came over me. I felt connected, warm, and comfortable. I had no future to consider, so I could be completely in the present." He felt truly alive for the first time. He laughed often at the irony that in order to fully live, he had to first give up on life.

After he suffered through chemotherapy and radiation treatment, the doctor told him he would most likely live. In that moment, Cees said, something curious happened: All the joy he had felt in the acceptance of death went away. Future entered his consciousness once again. Thoughts of, "What am I going to do now?" replaced the beauty, joy, and peace of his present awareness. This was the moment when his spiritual journey began. The question he pondered was, "How can I feel alive without needing to be told I'm going to die soon?"

I met Cees about eight years after he began that journey. He was now cancer-free. Over time, he had identified the mental constructs that had prevented him from being fully present with the joy of each moment. I was nowhere close to being able to do this. I was fumbling around in life, still stuck in my pain, insecurity, and self-identification. In Cees, I saw something missing in myself—a fire for life I remembered from my childhood, but that had long since disappeared.

Cees was obsessed with a grandiose vision. As he put it, "Before I die, I want to touch humanity with an experience that gives them the opportunity to decide whether they want to live free in spirit, or confined to a limiting self-identity."

As I mentioned, Cees was prone to take drastic action when he made a discovery. On one occasion, he realized many of his friends and family were coming to him for support when things got difficult. He would often assist them, then they would go away until the next challenge arose. For him, this was immensely dissatisfying because nothing was fundamentally changing in the people he tried to help. It was like putting a Band-Aid on a gaping wound.

He finally put a stop to this. He told everyone in his life, including family, "If you want to keep bringing your problems to me to fix, you need to pay me 10 percent of everything you earn for the rest of your life." This created a massive uproar, with his father calling to lecture him on appropriate behavior. Cees didn't care. He didn't play by societal rules of right or wrong. He just knew he was not happy with the situation and he was not going to settle for anything less.

There are two types of spiritual teachers: the ones who have more of a head awakening and those who have more of a heart awakening. You know which one you're having by paying attention to how you react to them. In the first case, you will feel closer to understanding yourself, and with the other you'll feel closer to the emotions that underlie your thoughts.

Cees was definitely a "heady" teacher. As such, his approach was far from gentle. Cees was confrontational to the point of ruthlessness. He would sit with people and ask them question after question, using their responses to dig what seemed like an eternal well to the soul. The questions were difficult to answer, and would normally end in hysterical laughter, followed by a tranquil state of silent and wondrous observation. The person would often feel that they had become wholly different in the exchange. The noise in their head had been turned off. The deeper voice of consciousness finally had a platform to speak from. It was a moment where the student had the opportunity to experience the self without the identification of who or what he or she *thought* they were. In that space, they discovered a pure state of being.

What I discovered was that pushing people so quickly to this point had its pitfalls. In general, two groups emerged: 1) the people who were happy to have had the experience and then were confused when it left, and 2) those who would come back over and over again to get a high, like a drug addict chasing another hit. In both cases, Cees would get frustrated. He was not looking to create a sect, nor did he want people dependent on him. He wanted each person to see that it never had to do with him or them, that there was something bigger than all of us, something that is often described as the state of oneness, or a non-dual state.

Through the questions he asked, Cees would almost always reach the moment where the person would be asked to see behind the eyes that were looking out. "Who is looking?" he would ask.

The person would often sit confused and answer, "Me."

"Who is 'me'?" he would continue.

Then the struggle would hit. The person would feel it first, usually with a quick smile, which would quickly go away, almost as if to say, "Oops, I can't open that door."

Cees would take the momentary expression as the cue that had they peeked and he would ask, "What did you just see?" He wouldn't give them the chance to deny they had seen into themselves. Then he would smile broadly. It was an open invitation saying, "I know you see it and I will sit here and smile until you join me here." It sometimes took a minute. It sometimes took an hour. But when it hit, the air felt full of electricity. Their eyes would get bigger, their whole bodies would open up, they would laugh. The laughter was contagious and would often continue for hours.

People would begin to see themselves as separate from their thoughts. They were no longer triggered to react. It was as if they were looking down on themselves from the corner of the room, laughing at how serious that poor person had made their life. They would smile broadly as if they had just tasted the most delicious cake. Eyes would move back and forth, scanning the room to see if others could also see it, as if to ask, "How could I have missed this all these years?" The laughter would continue and each word was no longer taken seriously. In fact, the question would arise, "Why am I speaking?" followed by a belly laugh that would often make observers confused and ask themselves, "What am I missing?"

Bathing in this space of non-identification was something new and people cherished it. Then inevitably, the identity would begin its struggle to take control back. It would often come in the subtlest of ways. The first question was almost always, "How do I not lose this?" Or, "How can I make sure to access this whenever I need it?"

At this moment, Cees would see the first signs that this wonderful state of "beginner's mind" was beginning to fade. He would be quick to share that this is not a state you go to. Rather, it emerges. He would say, "It shows up when you are not trying to get it to show up. But even that's not true, because you are then still trying to do something." This would be followed by more laughing.

This state is how life can be experienced when self-identity no longer colors everything you see. Being in this state is nothing more or less than sitting in silent observation of everything that is, including your own emotions. As Cees taught, "The emotions are as real as everything physical. Yet there is no reason to place value on them. Once that happens, you are no longer separate from the emotion—you *are* the emotion."

Cees was also quick to point out that emotions were not good nor bad. That would be placing judgment, which again confines the experience to the realm of what he called "personal." Cees loved the word "personal." It was the general category he used for any moment in which a person spoke without the awareness of how their emotions were governing their behavior and reactions. It was the moment when someone perceived the words of another as an attack, and then defended his or her beliefs or opinions.

In those moments, we don't listen to our inner voice, but we rather react to emotions in ourselves. We can know we're getting into the realm of "personal" when we start judging things as "right" or "wrong," "good" or "bad." We start playing "he said, she said" games. Of course, by labeling these moments as "personal," Cees was not judging them as good or bad, which would be an obvious contradiction. He simply pointed out, "When things get personal, we are no longer in a dialogue. We are no longer listening to one another. Instead, we are defending a point of view."

I had lost enough battles in my life by taking things personally, and I was starting to see the immense benefits of not doing that. I was applying this awareness around me and the benefits were clear. I was happy and healthy. I was learning and experimenting. I was no longer running away from problems in my life. I was walking directly in the middle and embracing it all. Life was good.

## CHAPTER 25

# FROM CORPORATE DIRECTOR TO UNEMPLOYED STUDENT

After experiencing Cees's training in my corporate job, I wanted more. In my case, the common saying, "When the student is ready, the teacher will appear," could not have been more true. I felt stranded on a desert island and Cees had both water and a boat. I was ready—to an extreme that few people in my life understood.

After ten years of working in my company, I quit and walked away. I sold all my possessions (and I do mean *all* of them) and moved into the attic space of Cees's apartment in Amsterdam. It was dark and damp. There was no plumbing or electricity. I would pee in a glass jar, or creep into Cees's home if more was required. We pulled an electrical cord up three stories so I could have electricity. The small window in the corner was both a blessing and a curse. I used a small space heater to combat the cold air that would rush through the cracks in the window pane.

I had gone from living in one of the nicest districts in one of the best cities in the world, to this. I had gone from being a corporate director to being unemployed. You might think I had gone insane, as many people thought. Yet I have never felt more alive than I did then. I had spent so many years building up material things and distractions that I was struck by how easy life can be when it's all gone.

A line from Janis Joplin's song, *Me and Bobby McGee*, kept running through my mind: "Freedom's just another word for nothing left to lose." I thought of the story of putting a frog in tepid water, then slowly bringing it to a boil until the frog dies. I did not know that, in my corporate job, I had been gradually boiling myself to death. The money, the status, and the idea of who I was had been killing me slowly.

As I was struggling to leave my emotionally dead-end job, I had been looking for opportunities outward. I scanned the market for something that could replace everything I didn't like about my current position. I was in a rut and I expected a new job could change this.

After complaining for about three years, I noticed a list of excuses that came up when I was considering change. Things like, "You are so respected that it would be crazy to leave." Or, "You are paid so well that it would be risky in a place they don't know you." It made it impossible to find a job that would satisfy all the anxieties of my inner voice. What I soon noticed was that behind the voice was fear: the fear of not knowing, the fear that I might fail. The fear that the man I imagined myself to be might prove unsuccessful.

In this tension of these first few weeks of dramatic change, Cees taught me one of life's great lessons: There is a critical difference between making a choice and making a decision. In fact, it dawned on me that I may never have made a decision in my life.

Cees spent a lot of time discussing such distinctions. He loved the word "distinction." He often said, "If you do not have a clear distinction, then you do not have a clear understanding." Before teaching, he asked me, "What is the difference between a choice and a decision?"

I sat and looked at him, not really knowing what to say.

Then he began teaching: "The distinction is subtle, but like many lessons in life, transformational. Life has always presented you with choices. You graduated high school and you had a choice of colleges. You went out for entertainment and you had a choice of movies. You went to the job market and you had a choice of positions. Your life has been an endless number of choices that appeared to you as freedom. And the question arises: Have you ever really had free will, or is it just an illusion?"

Confused, I asked, "But couldn't you consider those choices to come from me?"

He laughed and continued, "Of course. But to what degree were those choices laid out for you? To what degree have you been following a path you believed was your own, all while barriers were being placed to the left and right of you to make sure you stayed somewhere in the middle?"

I thought about all the lessons that I had learned throughout my travels, and I knew he was right. Yet I still did not completely understand the distinction he was pointing at. He asked again, "So what is the difference between a choice and decision?"

Again I was unable to answer.

He continued, "It's quite simple. When you make a decision in life, it excludes future choices. Or put differently, if you are not excluding something in the future, it is still a choice. So in making a decision, you burn a bridge behind you. You don't leave yourself the option to go back."

I was coming to grips with a strange paradox: Creativity emerges by making decisions that force you to start thinking beyond the obvious choices. Before understanding this, I was full of fear and anxiety regarding my job situation. I was looking for alternative choices, not knowing that I first had to make the decision to leave my work. This reminded me again of the moment my father threw me out and I looked in the mirror and said, "I'm not going to accept this." But this time, instead of being forced to make a decision, I had made one on my own timetable.

Leaving my job with no certainty about what I would do afterward was my first real decision in life—at least as far as I can remember. It was the first time I did not follow one of the predetermined options before me. And that was when blood began to circulate through my veins again. I finally felt alive again.

Cees once said something I'll never forget: "Freedom is the absence of choice." These are words I hold dear. The clearer I find my life today, the more I see that my past decisions (or the things I say no to) dictate fewer and fewer choices that are available to me. I often hear the word "principle" used to describe this. By excluding certain choices, my life was becoming easier to navigate and I was becoming more consistent.

This may be best understood by sharing a coaching situation. Cees and I were working with a CEO who posed a problem. He said, "I was asked by an employee to remain quiet about something she wanted to tell me, and I agreed. Afterward, I found myself compromised when the issue she shared pertained to my relationship with another person. What should I do?"

Cees responded, "I would have never allowed myself to be in that situation to begin with." The CEO was puzzled. Cees continued, "I never would have accepted the condition that I would be able to remain quiet. How could I? If I were to accept this condition, I would be unreliable and unable to be genuine with others." He went on to give him an alternative: "I would have said, 'As long as what you tell me does not happen to compromise my contact with anyone or things that need to get done here, then fine, I can agree to not ever share it.'"

The speed and clarity of Cees' reply was based on a decision he had made years before: "I will not allow anything in my life that would possibly undermine my relationships with others." This may seem obvious on paper, but it is almost never obvious at the moment. People want to say yes quickly without really knowing what they are saying yes to. That's precisely why decisions are critical and have impact, even many years later.

Now, in the attic space of Cees's apartment, I found real freedom in my decision to leave my job. As you might expect, this dramatic shift created quite a stir. My friends were very suspicious of my new direction. On one occasion, I had lunch with a friend, Michael. He was a very logical graphic designer who was quick to tell you his opinions as "facts."

"Andy," he said, "you do not know what you are doing. People like this Cees guy are dangerous."

I did my best to explain my reasoning for the change, but Michael was adamant that something was wrong. He was so convinced that he said emphatically, "You'll see and you'll come back to me and tell me I was right."

I noticed that as I changed, people had trouble interacting with me. I would try and share what was important for me and people could not identify with any of it. They kept waiting for the "real" Andy to show up so they could have talks like we used to. But I was no longer interested in talking about people and things. I had nothing new to discover there. I was full of wonder. The thoughts that occupied me were things like: How do we form into the beings we have become? What are the parts of me that are based on past patterns and what are the ones that are defined today? Is there free will or am I just the byproduct of learned behaviors from the past? Why do we have the need to believe in a God?

The people who had learned to like the more free-spirited version of Andy worried about me now. My friend Thomas, a consultant, told me flat-out that he didn't like who I was becoming. I was shocked because I was full of happiness and excitement. I was hurt that he would not be happy for me. I wanted everyone to ask me, "But are you happy?" If they had only asked, they would have realized the truth of things.

Instead of sharing my joy with others, I felt as if I constantly needed to defend my actions—as if I was responsible to them for who I was becoming. I needed to appease their insecurity that I was still the Andy they knew, at least in their eyes. The lesson I took away from this experience is that people are always projecting on to one another. When we see things we don't like in other people, we are seeing things we don't like and accept in ourselves. To gain a sense of security, we want others to live according to our opinions and beliefs. If one person in the relationship no longer matches the projection of the other, it causes problems.

I was seeing firsthand how people keep one another in line by making sure they fulfill the expectations that they have of each other. I was slowly moving away from the way I was defined by society, and moving toward to a definition of my own. Who that person was, I was just beginning to know.

What I did know is that I was getting less and less worried about what other people thought about me. I didn't try to appease others. Rather, I was heartfelt and honest, even if others found that honesty difficult to handle at times. I got in tune with an empathy I had been aware I had all the way back to childhood. I was just starting to figure out how to balance my deep emotions in a business setting. Now the question was, how could I be the person I wanted to be in any environment?

## CHAPTER 26
# EMBRACING MY EMOTIONS WITHOUT RESISTANCE

After working with Cees, I had a deeper self-awareness than ever before. I began realizing that, as I came to peace with aspects of myself, I could help others with the same challenges. Now I had to figure out how I was going to bring this to the world in the way that was natural to me.

My honesty was often met with surprise, as I would say things others were thinking, but were afraid to freely express. I began to hold less and less judgment for myself, and therefore for others. I remembered my mother calling me her "little shit-stirrer." But now, by speaking boldly to people, I was not looking to cause trouble, but rather create opportunities for connection.

What I came to see is that we judge in others the things we

refuse to see and accept in ourselves. Or, we actually become the very thing we judge in others. In my case, the clearest example of this was my father. Because of his rage, I vowed to never follow in his footsteps. I would never raise my voice at others because that was not right. I sat in judgment of him and thereby became the victim of my own judgment.

This showed up most obviously in my relationships with girlfriends. I would let weeks or months pass without acknowledging difficulties I was having with them. Inevitably, there would be a straw that broke the camel's back and I would explode, at times with even greater intensity than my father. One time, I overheard my girlfriend speaking with a man on the phone in a voice that sounded more than just casual. She and I had spoken about the issue a few times previously, and now I had reached my limit. I fell into a rage. I was angry that she was not willing to admit her betrayal and that she was lying to my face. I yelled and yelled at her.

Once you have gone that far, there's no turning back. People you have treated that way never trust you again. Once you have shown the capacity to be that vicious, people will always live in fear that it could happen again. It was devastating to me to realize I had become my father.

I remember that as a child I would walk upstairs in the house, above the room where my father worked. I would tread lightly so as not to wake the sleeping giant. This memory is seared into my mind: the scared little boy walking up the stairs as if walking on hot coals. Now all the people in my life were walking on those same hot coals, trying not to get burned.

This is when I called everyone I thought I might have hurt to apologize. I even called my father to share the discovery with him. Since I didn't express judgment toward him in sharing it, he was open to hearing it. I shared the fear I had felt walking up the stairs and he said, "And you never knew what would set it off!"

When I heard these words, my stomach dropped. He had just revealed that he had been aware of his own emotional state and he was also aware that it was beyond reason. He was able to acknowledge that he had not been able to control his own emotions.

In this process of healing, I learned an important lesson: Anger is good. In fact, it's great. It's just as important an emotion as happiness. When I suppressed anger, the lesson it was trying to teach me was not able to reveal itself. Behind all my anger was fear and insecurity, the need to feel safe, respected, and loved. The need for belonging. For most of my life, I used anger to cover up my vulnerability, because it made me feel weak. Now, instead of judging my anger and suppressing it, I began to look beyond it to see the truth and beauty of my raw humanity.

I discovered that my judgment of good and bad greatly inhibited my ability to embrace life in all its fullness and richness. Anger, like love, hope, or sadness, is just another human emotion that has every right to exist alongside other emotional states. Yet I had judged anger as a "negative" emotion, and even blamed those who expressed it. I hadn't distinguished between the emotion itself and a violent, physical expression of it, which had been such a negative aspect of my upbringing.

One of my greatest breakthroughs was fully embracing the things in my father I had judged for so long. I no longer thought anger should be avoided. (By the same token, neither should it be encouraged.) I just accepted it as a place where I sometimes found myself. And in that acceptance, something completely new emerged. I was no longer holding back my emotions, so I had far fewer explosions. And when the explosions did come, I was able to embrace what they were telling me.

Anger, like all emotions, is telling us something—and it is usually quite right in its observation. Where we tend to fail is in our *interpretation* of it. My emotions were speaking to me, and I was starting to listen closer than ever before. I felt as if my stomach was like one of those heart monitor machines in hospitals that beep with every heartbeat and show the moving line on the screen. My emotions were just little beeps on the readout. Certain life events set off larger blips. I was now beginning to feel the blips and heighten my consciousness around them. Instead of reacting to them, I would ask, "What is this blip trying to tell me?"

As I trained myself to listen, I could now hear the underlying message. Over time, it has become like listening to an old friend.

The more I sat in quiet observation, the more the voice shared. What I discovered about cultivating the voice is that forcing myself to speak before thinking too much revealed a lot. It was as if the voice was ready to say what was on its mind, but the brain wanted to filter it. The voice was ready to blurt it out and the mind was worried how others might take it, or that the speaker (me) might be left vulnerable.

In the past, I used sarcasm to conceal my inner voice. This sarcasm has slowly turned into love and connection. Although in my work I ask people to be vulnerable, I often find myself balancing somewhere between humor and pain. I am never quite sure how much vulnerability will be allowed, or how much safety there is in the group and how quickly it can change. I'm constantly with one foot on the gas (my desire to be open and vulnerable) and another foot on the brake (my desire to create a feeling of safety).

Something else was also becoming clear to me: my emotional "heart monitor" had a "limiter" on it. I saw that in suppressing any single emotion, all the other emotions were suppressed alongside it. For instance, when I did not allow my sadness to be embraced, my happiness never quite surpassed the point that sadness reached. The consequence was a dampening of all of my emotional states—the gray and dull life I had created for myself in Austria.

To break out of this state, I had to do something scary. I had to feel again. And not just *think about* my feelings, as I had done so well in Australia with Matthew, but *be* those feelings. I could no longer chip away slowly at the protective layer I had built around my heart. I needed to get out the jackhammer. It was now time to smash my wall into pieces and see what was underneath it, warts and all.

I wish I could say that once I had this realization, I acted immediately. But I cannot. I was scared. I had been hurt so many times before, and vulnerability did not come easy. But I did begin to take bigger risks and open my heart more. As I did so, the blips on the line of my "heart monitor" were shooting higher and lower. The high points of joy and the low points of sadness reminded me of the beauty in vulnerability.

Over the years, my peace with my own emotions has grown. Having said that, the start of dealing with any emotion is always challenging. Take anger, for example. As I mentioned, I vowed early on not to be like my father. If you had met me before I learned to embrace my emotions, you might not have seen anger in me. In fact, you would have only seen anger if you'd thought counterintuitively, "Andy is far too happy and open. He must be suppressing something. No one can be that flexible."

What I have experienced, time after time, is a pendulum swing between emotion and rationality. When I have suppressed any emotion, it always eventually manifests in unhealthy ways. What I've learned to do is allow my emotions to express themselves. Then, as they feel welcome in me, they no longer fight to get out so much, and I'm able to be present with them in more balanced ways. When we allow emotions, we are no longer defined solely by them. It's presumptuous to think we can grow beyond our emotions. But what we can do is allow them and observe them as they are. This gives us space to respond to them differently.

For example, one time, after I had accepted my anger, I was on a phone call with a friend. He was making certain assumptions: "Andy, I know you are seeing things through the eyes of a marketer. If you only understood how a coder works . . ." Normally, I would have allowed people to speak to me like this. But this time, I let my emotions out without guard or self-judgment. I was not going to allow someone to dismiss my suggestion based on an assumption. I yelled and yelled at him. He yelled back, which was not something he was accustomed to doing.

The strange thing was, I felt a sense of peace. I allowed myself to lose control over something I had spent so much of my life bottling up. I had finally allowed myself anger, without judgment.

This does not mean that there were no consequences. The next day I called my friend to apologize for the harshness in my voice. But I felt no regret for my words. I had given anger a home and it was no longer being suppressed.

What I have found is that when an emotion is no longer suppressed, it no longer comes out as an explosion. It integrates into psyche. That does not mean that there are not moments of anger, but they are felt so much in the moment that they tend to dissipate quite quickly. And, as I've said, anger is a great clue. When I am angry, I know there is something going on that needs to stop. By feeling the anger, and not only being angry, I have written some incredible complaint letters.

This process of allowing emotion to explode, and then giving it a home, is what I call "grounding." Suppressed emotions are like neglected, insecure children—constantly acting out and fighting for attention and love in obnoxious and socially unpleasant ways. When we welcome them into our hearts and give them a home, a place of belonging, essentially they "settle down." They no longer act out in unhealthy ways because they feel a sense of belonging. They no longer have a need to get out or be seen. This means they can simply "be" without any tension of resistance. In this sense, another word for "grounding" could be "allowing."

I have found this process of grounding to be remarkably predictable. At first, I am so overwhelmed with my own emotion that I can't spend any time with it. I resist and suppress. Then, I allow it—both in terms of resting in me, as well as expressing itself with others. When I first start allowing it to express itself, it's immature and messy. It can often make others uncomfortable, or even offend people. Then, as I accept and love it, even when it is at its worst, it calms down. Its outward expressions tend to be more mature and peaceful. And finally, the more I accept the emotion within myself, the more I am able to have empathy for it in others.

A simple example may be useful. In the past, when telemarketers would call me and try to sell products to me, I would immediately get triggered and bark, "I did not ask for your call. Please don't call back."

Now, when I hear a salesperson desperate to make a deal, it gives me energy. I see how I am no different than this person in different areas of my life. I feel compassion and I have the ability to interact with him or her in a way that creates connection. I will often say to telemarketers, "Thank you for calling. You have a terribly difficult job and, although I am not interested, I appreciate the effort you are making." This is often met with surprise and appreciation. Now that I have nothing to protect, there is a wonderful opportunity to allow the person's neediness into my system because I am no longer defending against it. At the same time, it does not need to stay there. So once I hang up the phone, I am left with an appreciation for that aspect of myself.

The degree to which I have grounded an emotion within myself is the degree to which I can invite the same emotion from others. I see that emotional triggers reveal places in me where I have the most room to grow. Instead of avoiding those emotions, I welcome them in and allow the pendulum to swing to the other side for a while.

In my first few years with Cees, as I connected with my deepest sadness, I saw something incredible happen: I was beginning to build meaningful relationships with others. It became so clear that sharing emotions with others created deep connections.

I had changed. I was once a dam, holding back any emotion I judged as negative or inappropriate. Now, I was turning into an ocean—waves of happiness and sadness washed over me and then back into the sea from which they came. I was stripping away my layers of fear and self-deception to see things in myself I had never seen before.

But the greatest lesson I was learning was to see the falsehood in my self-identity. I had observed identity in others through my years of traveling. But I had never quite seen through my own identity. I wasn't even sure to what degree that was possible.

What I was keenly aware of was that this was not a journey I could make on my own. As much as Cees had already impacted me, I had much more to learn from him.

# CHAPTER 27
# BEYOND RIGHT AND WRONG

After being mentored by Cees for about a year, I partnered with him in starting a business. We wanted to help other people experience the same breakthroughs I had worked through, to help them see beyond the limits of self-identity, to learn how to find meaning and joy in pain. Cees had already been doing corporate training, so that's where we wanted to focus our business.

Cees and his wife, Kai, owned a restaurant below the house we lived in. The three of us would often meet there to discuss our plans. Cees had lofty visions. He was an idealist. He was a good marketer for others, but not for himself. When I came to work with him, the name he used for his corporate coaching and consulting business was "Not the Carrot." It was a mysterious name designed to invoke the obvious question, "If it's not the carrot, then is it the stick?"

In that name, Cees was trying to encompass an idea of how the brain works. He saw that the dichotomy between right and wrong was false. The carrot and the stick pointed at that binary perspective. When he was asked a question that was placed in the context of right and wrong, he would often say, "It's not that I'm not saying that." He loved the use of the double negative. It was his way of saying you are correct, and at the same time you have more to see. It was a way of not triggering the negative reaction in the other person, and opening the door to a wider dialogue. Sometimes it would come, sometimes it wouldn't.

So we spent a lot of time naming what we did. Every few months or so, Cees would come up with another company name, and I would spend the next few days working non-stop to create a logo and website, everything required to create a public face. This went on for about six years until I finally said, "No." What I realized was that the name of our business was not why our clients were coming to us. In fact, most didn't even know our name, because we had changed it so many times.

So I finally said, "We are going to pick a simple, boring name so that none of our clients will need to give it a thought." For us, it was always about creating meaningful relations, so that's the name we stuck with: Meaningful Relations.

We had a hard time growing because Cees had several criteria for the companies we would work with. When the tax department of the Netherlands came to us asking for a training on interpersonal relations, Cees said we could not work for an organization that uses force to coerce its clients. When the manager from an IT company came telling us he wanted us to help his group, Cees said the group was not the problem. Rather, it was the manager's ability to lead it.

We did get a few clients, but Cees was always looking to make an impact with everyone he met. Sometimes people just wanted a simple service. For Cees, every training needed to turn into a life-changing event. That meant we made some incredible contacts, but for the most part people did not know how to deal with us. We did not fit into the conventional box of "trainer" they were looking for.

The single criteria we used to define what we did or did not do was, "Does it make us happy?" If we felt more happiness, we continued. If we felt less happiness, we brought it to the person we were working with to see if we could figure something out. Slowly we built a following and learned alongside each other. We stumbled from one failure to another, embracing it all as an overwhelming success.

Cees was not always easy for me to be around. He was obsessed with consciousness, and he would spend hours discussing the distinctions between different levels, and the criteria for each. I would record each conversation and we built a library of hours of material that he would never actually use.

Cees was very clear that we human beings have an identity, which defines us in our language. He was very precise about language. He said, "It is through our words that we demonstrate our state of being in the world. By stating things in a more personal form, we are confined to the definition we create of ourselves."

It made him crazy when I would use language sloppily. For example, I would say something like, "I am not good in teaching groups."

He would be quick to stop that mode of speaking. "Andy," he would say, "in saying that you are not good at it, you are defining yourself as not good at it. This holds you captive in a box of self-identity. You are no longer free to choose who you become. What you *can* say is that you do not observe yourself doing that well."

This was not a play in semantics: it was a fundamentally different way of experiencing the world. In the latter, Cees was quick to point out that in simply observing it, you are free to redefine it. You can become whatever or whomever you'd like. You have no need to create an idea or conceptualization of yourself. If you simply observe yourself, you have all the freedom to learn, grow, and change into something completely different—even moment by moment.

Cees was also very clear that he believed one could achieve virtually anything when one was not defined by the self-identity. He was cautious to use the word "ego" because it was often filled with a heavy load of judgment. He would always say that the ego is not necessarily a bad thing. We should not think in terms of trying to overcome our egos, a trap he witnessed in other spiritual teachings. Rather, we should heighten our consciousness around the ego so that we are no longer defined and confined to it. This is why he didn't like to hear the words, "I am . . . "

He taught me to experience life. He would often say that he did not want me to base my understanding on his experience, but rather on my own. "To do that," he said, "you will need to learn the difference between having thoughts and thinking." He explained that everyone has thoughts, but very few people actually think.

This was a curious distinction for me. I began to see that my head was always buzzing with noise—a stream of consciousness that generated thought after thought. Cees once said to me, "Try to think a thought before you think it. It's impossible!" This was a remarkable insight that revealed that I did not control my own thoughts. The only thing I did control is what I did with those thoughts.

He went on to say, "If you think about it, this key insight carries the potential to release you from the prison of your mind. If you accept that your thoughts are random, then why are you taking them so seriously? Why not just accept that whatever your mind produces is just static and you do not need to get lost in it? Like a cable TV network with thousands of stations, you can flip through it and decide what you want to watch. You are not a victim of it."

I saw it. I was aware of the thoughts, but I had never imagined they could be simply ignored. I asked myself, *Who would I be without my thoughts?*

Cees left me with a final statement, "You don't decide what the programming is going to be, but you do decide what to focus on. If you are flipping through channels, then you are being driven by thoughts. If you focus on good programming and start thinking, you'll see how things change quickly."

I never before considered the quality of my thoughts, nor the relevance to the people I was with. This meant that I would share random thoughts, which could distract from the matter at hand. I was not observing the process in myself. Rather, I was blindly feeding it with content. I was reacting to my thoughts rather than thinking about their relevance, where they were coming from, or how they might support the situation I found myself in. Once I no longer took my thoughts seriously, I was able to see them all as possibilities.

The difference for Cees was critical because it exhausted him to interact with people's thoughts. As soon as discussions turned into two people transferring information to one another, Cees would check out. When people would say, "I think . . . " followed by an opinion, he would ask them to rephrase it by saying, "In my experience . . . " and then share what they had witnessed.

He was in a constant search for what he called "meaningful relations." He defined this in the distinction between discussing and having a dialogue. For him, a dialogue was the moment two people meet in consciousness. In a dialogue, there are no ideas of right and wrong defining the interaction. There is simply the quest to interact with one another and one's self simultaneously. You listen to how the words of the other impact you and allow yourself to be fully seen, without guard, in that response.

Cees saw that growth could only come through vulnerability. At the same time, he saw that vulnerability was one of the hardest things for people to allow. Most of the people Cees would interact with were not capable of accessing this vulnerability in themselves. It would often come out masked in some level of protection.

On one occasion, a man in a training began to complain that Cees's approach was not suitable for groups. The customer interjected, "What you are doing is not made for businesses. You are better doing this in one-on-one sessions."

Cees was never quick to take a side, so he asked him, "What is wrong with vulnerability in the business?"

He responded, "There is a work life and home life, and they need to remain separate."

Cees acknowledged the truth in the statement and then asked again, "So what are you afraid of?"

"Nothing," the client retorted.

The back and forth continued until the inevitable occurred:

Cees pointed out how the trainee moved away from discomfort and tried to hide it.

The man saw the point and laughed. Cees gave him freedom to speak, and he said, "I just don't trust this environment." He then shared a story of years of disappointment and frustration. He had not trusted himself to be vulnerable because he had been disappointed so many times before. He had shut down. Now, Cees was trying to open the box that had been sealed years earlier.

When I first met Cees, I was no different than anyone in his trainings. One of the first tasks Cees gave me was to read Karl Popper's book, *Conjectures and Refutations*. It was one of those long, dreadful books you get assigned in college and ask yourself, "How will this help me in real life?" It was heavy and dense and chock-full of references. I turned to the last page to see how many pages I had to count down. Then I began reading.

It took me a while to find my stride, but then something beautiful emerged: I began to see my life before my eyes. I saw a struggle I had lived with for years: the fight between right and wrong. I saw that there were always two sides to a story, and because I was often capable of seeing both, I would get stuck.

What is truth? Strange as it may sound, this question was at the heart of many of the complications I encountered with people. Once I accepted that there was truth, I was immediately at odds with anyone who did not also share that truth.

I remember in college getting into a heated battle with someone regarding the death of John F. Kennedy. It was just after the Oliver Stone film had come out and I was completely willing to accept the conclusions of the film without any further exploration. I lived with an engineer who clearly had a more disciplined thinking process, and I was comfortable parroting the arguments made in the movie, almost as if I were its star character. What I learned is that speaking of truth is confining for me. It requires that I constantly shore up my arguments, and eventually leads to a separation within myself, and between myself and others.

Popper presented me with an alternative that I had never thought possible—seeing two sides is the problem to begin with. It never dawned on me that I was playing by the rules society dictated. As soon as I accepted there was right and wrong, I was confined to the dichotomy this creates. In a nutshell, Popper said there is no absolute truth. Nothing can be said as fact.

This was at odds with everything I had learned in college. The scientific method was created for that very purpose—so we could make hypotheses and test them, and in that testing, come to objective conclusions. But according to Popper, all we can ever do is make a statement and define the context in which the statement is true. For example, the statement, "Water boils at 212 degrees Fahrenheit." In scientific terms, this would be true. But Popper would point out that the statement can only be true if conditions are added. For example, "Water boils at 212 degrees *if* the water has no sodium content and it is boiled at sea level." Otherwise, the statement is not true.

All this philosophical blabbing may seem abstract. But I saw it had far-reaching consequences in my personal life. It turned my thinking upside down. Before reading Popper's book, I was living in the land of right and wrong, the land of "he said, she said." Afterwards, I was sitting with a new reality: *Everyone was right all the time.* Like Popper, they define the context for the statement they are making. Knowing this, how can I disagree with anything?

If someone calls me an idiot, they are in fact correct. What I do not know is the context they have for saying that. Of course, this does not mean that I am *only* an idiot. It just means they have a context in which that statement is true.

In this awareness, I became full of questions. I was no longer interested in proving my point to be correct, but rather in what context the other was considering when making his or her statement. If I ever found myself conflicted, it would be resolved in the discovery of the context. If someone said something I disagreed with or didn't understand, or if I felt myself reacting, I would just sit in wonder about the context they must be referring to. In what context is their statement true? The only way I could figure out the context was by asking genuinely curious questions.

I stopped defending or trying to convince people of my position. Instead, I would simply ask, "What makes you say that?" I looked for the context for their statements. Thus, I found myself learning from each discussion. Instead of getting more set in my ways, I was learning to flow freely. I was learning to listen closely and create very meaningful relationships, even with people I never thought possible.

I was feeling more and more confident. I was inviting things in that had once been unheard of. After a long hiatus, it was now time to reacquaint myself with my father. I was less curious how he would be after all those years and more curious who I would be with him after all the years of my development.

## CHAPTER 28

# RECONCILIATION

At this point in my life, I had not seen my father in over ten years. The last time I had seen him was when he threw me out of the house and disowned me. But after I had called him to share some of my discoveries with him, the door to reconciliation had opened.

On our call he had said, "It would be nice to meet." I agreed, and he arranged to visit me in Amsterdam. As I sat in the airport waiting for his arrival, my mind rushed with thoughts. I didn't know my father at this stage of his life, nor did I know who I would be with him. He walked through the gate with a big smile on his face. I walked up to him and we embraced. No tears, just a loving hug. It felt as if we both weren't sure what our relationship was going to become.

I drove him to Amsterdam, then took him to the small boat Cees had let sit in front of his house for ten years. It was an old plastic thing about the size of a bathtub that comfortably seats one, and two less comfortably. I wanted to give him an experience, and it was a nice way to break the ice. I rowed the boat through the canals to his hotel, which was on the water. I started questioning my decision when I realized how difficult it would be to get him and his luggage off the small boat, but a woman on a nearby houseboat saw our dilemma and waved us over. It was as if she knew this was an important moment and sensed I wanted to get it right. She helped us unload the luggage.

After getting my father situated at his hotel, I spent the next few hours walking with him along the canals of Amsterdam. He had become frail since I had last seen him. He no longer exuded the strength he once had. He was just an old man walking cautiously on the cobblestone streets.

We slowly began speaking about the past. As painful or potentially threatening topics came up, I would embrace his interpretation of events, then share a broader perspective on how it might be possible to view it. He told me how lost I was and how my choices in life were leading to dangerous areas. I acknowledged that he had a point, and then slowly shared that, apparently, I needed to go through that to get to where I was now.

I could see he was getting accustomed to interacting with someone new. Whenever he would bring forward subjects that could get emotional, I would always allow the space for us to have a dialogue. I never reacted with an idea of good and bad.

At one point he said, "Your mother was a real cunt."

I fell back, amazed. Normally, that would have set me off and a major argument would have ensued. But this time, I simply felt confused that I did not need to defend her, nor my feelings for her. And at the same time, I was able to be there for him. As if I was comforting someone with whom I had no association, I simply said, "Wow, she died so many years ago. What are you still holding onto?"

He saw the sincerity in my eyes. He had nothing to fight against. He began to cry and shared the regret of how he had dealt with her after the divorce. I sat in quiet observation. There was nothing to say. It was the pain he needed to go through.

Later that evening, I hit my first emotional hurdle. As we walked the streets, he decided he wanted to eat one of the famous "space cakes" (marijuana-infused brownies) from Amsterdam. Although I was not happy at the prospect, I decided to stay with him, which turned into a terrible mistake.

After he finished eating the cake, it took about forty-five minutes for the effects to start kicking in. We walked in the busy Leidseplein area of Amsterdam along the restaurants with the all-you-can-eat ribs. As we passed a table, he asked a man how the ribs were.

The man replied, "Great! Want to try one?"

The next thing I knew, my father was reaching down to pick up one of the ribs from his plate. It reminded me of my ten-year-old self. When I was a child, my father would often send me to the local department stores to return things he had bought and worn for years, but no longer used. The store he liked most was Nordstrom's. On one occasion, I took a pair of shoes he had worn for more than ten years to the store to return them. When I went to the counter, I felt a deep sense of shame.

I put the shoes on the counter and said, "I'd like a refund." I explained that I was sent by my father and I was not happy I had to do this. I also said, "I wish you would change your return policy so I wouldn't have to go through this." The cashier seemed sympathetic to my discomfort and smiled. I felt a great sense of relief.

My father liked putting me in these uncomfortable situations. As soon as I saw the rib in his mouth, I felt as if my childhood was rising up inside of me. When I got home, I couldn't sleep. I knew something was wrong but I couldn't put my finger on it. Then I felt the ten-year-old in me. I saw my childhood before my eyes. I was now stuck.

I had allowed myself to get into an uncomfortable situation. The issue wasn't with the drugs, nor taking the rib, but his behavior I had been unable to deal with as a child. When I was a child, my father could behave any way he wanted to. He could do things that made me feel hurt, scared, or embarrassed and I had no power to do anything about it. As an adult, I did not yet know how to set boundaries. Prior to this situation, I always had had one of two reactions: I would either shut down emotionally, or lash out aggressively. Now, he was perfectly free to behave any way he wanted—but I wasn't yet able to reconcile that with what I wanted.

I met with Cees in the morning and he told me very clearly, "You need to set boundaries on what is and is not acceptable to you. You cannot compromise now or you'll never be able to recover."

I felt the weight of the earth on my shoulders. I hadn't refused when my father asked to eat the brownie, so I was also responsible. I was anxious to make a boundary around something I had just permitted. I knew that if I did not confront this head-on, it would fester and erode the progress I made over the past few years.

In the past, "setting boundaries" for me would have been a very defensive reaction. Furthermore, it would have been irresponsible—it would have been placing blame on the other person. It would have been inferring that the other person was at fault and putting him in his place. Now, I saw that the problem is never with other people—it's always something in myself that I haven't dealt with. With this new understanding, I realized that setting boundaries was about me owning up to my own issues. It wasn't about what my father had done wrong—it was about what I was or wasn't willing to accept. In this context, it became a very conscious, loving, and responsible act.

So after meeting with Cees, I told my father I wanted to have a talk with him. I asked him if we could take a walk. He could sense it was serious. Because of his manic nature, most people in his life had refused contact with him. His sister and a list of others had already said he was not permitted to call them anymore.

We walked and found a bench to sit on. My heart was pounding. I told him I was sorry about what had happened the previous night. I told him I wasn't happy about it, and that I wouldn't allow it to happen again. I said, "It's not your problem. It was my problem for not taking responsibility. From now on, I will take responsibility when I'm feeling uncomfortable. It was my inability, so there's nothing you need to feel uncomfortable about."

He looked at me with solemn eyes and said, "Well, I guess that's that." Because he had gotten so used to being rejected and people shutting him out of their lives, he was interpreting my words as me rejecting him. In his mind, by me saying this, it meant we probably would never see each other again.

I laughed and said, "It's not that I want to end our relationship. It's just that I can't allow this to happen again." I repeated, "You weren't at fault. I just need you to know that in the future, I won't let that happen again."

We then both smiled and relaxed. I believe that was the first time he actually felt like he could trust me. I was willing to tell him how it was for me without blaming him for my discomfort. There was a strange shift in our relationship. It was no longer hierarchical. Just as I had experienced with my Aunt Ann, we became equals. We spent the next week together in London. We went from musical to musical and laughed for days. It was one of the last times I would be with my father, and it was special for both of us.

At dinner, in the London hotel where we were staying, I thanked him for all he had given me. As he had given me very little financial support and hadn't paid for my college, he looked at me with confusion and said, "I paid for both of your brothers to go to law school." The connection between love and money was very strong for him.

I said, "I'm not talking about financial support. When I was wandering the world and not sure where to go, you gave me exactly what I needed. By kicking me out of the house, you set me free. From that moment forward I was in charge of my own life. And you made that possible."

Both of us had eyes full of tears. He had never been thanked for the part of him he had struggled with most of his life: his manic rages. He thanked me for sharing, and then quickly turned the conversation back to the only way he knew how to love: through his financial support. He said, "If you ever want to become a lawyer, let me know and I'd be happy to pay for your education."

I laughed and said, "Thank you, but I've already found my calling."

The next day, I dropped him off at the airport and watched

him cross through the metal detector, waiting in line to pass through customs. I was holding on to the moment, knowing every moment I saw him could be the last one. I realized that after all these years of not having time with him, I would at some point lose him forever. I felt both grateful and sad—grateful that I had found this place with him, and sad that it would not last forever.

Thankfully, my life had also taken a turn romantically. In learning to love myself, I was also learning how to love someone else.

## CHAPTER 29
# I FIND MY SOUL MATE

**W**hen I arrived in Amsterdam, I was not looking for a relationship. I had screwed up enough of them in the past that I realized it was time for me to work on the relationship with myself before introducing someone else into the picture.

In a chance website visit, I posted my profile on an expatriate webpage in Amsterdam. I was very clear in my posting: "I am not looking for a relationship." Not long afterward, I received a message with an invitation to meet from a woman named Rani. It was holiday season and I was alone in Amsterdam. I thought, "What better opportunity is there to have Christmas dinner with someone I have never met?"

On Christmas Eve, I drove an hour to the Hague where we had a wonderful evening in a typical café. It was simple Dutch cuisine, and the company was unforgettable. Rani was a dark-haired woman from Indonesia with a reserved nature. We sat and spoke for about three hours.

It felt less like a date and more like meeting an old friend. I didn't feel the sparks of sexual energy I was familiar with. My heart did not go pitter-patter. I did not lose myself in the moment. I did not think, "This is going to be the woman I spend the rest of my life with." I just felt I had met someone beautiful in her own right. I felt gratified that I'd met someone with whom I enjoyed spending time.

I had to leave dinner at 9 p.m. to pick up Cees from the airport. But I was quite certain Rani and I would meet again. Up until that point, love had always been an event for me. There was a moment I fell in love and it blinded me to all the qualities that would later ruin the relationship. I was looking for a high, for something that could fill the void of what was missing in my heart. This had happened on many occasions. But this time it was different. I was not guided by sexual energy. I was attracted to who I was with this person. I immediately saw that I became a better person when we were together.

From the beginning, we both realized how different we were from each other. She had a degree in Econometrics and was well-versed in advanced economic theories. She had always been incredibly determined. She always had dreams that were bigger than Indonesia. At the age of seventeen, without telling her parents, she took a bus to Jakarta, about three hours away from her home, to take an exam that offered scholarships to students with the highest scores. She scored at the top of her area. Eventually she told her parents she had decided to move to the Netherlands to study.

When we met, it was clear to me that she had a deep desire to understand how things work on an intellectual level. In contrast, I was often led by my feelings. We have often had long talks about how the mind works. I ask her to look inside of herself and see what she finds, while she listens to TED videos and shares the latest findings in science with me. We've never stopped growing independently as well as together.

For our first six years of dating, we spent time commuting back and forth between Amsterdam and the Hague. Every

Friday night, I would pick up Rani at the train station on my moped. We always looked forward to the weekend. We still call Friday our date night. Then, when Rani's apartment flooded during a heavy rain season, we decided she would move in with me. That meant that she had an hour-long commute to and from her office in the Hague.

It took a bit of adjusting for us to find our rhythm together. Rani was a founder of a hedge fund, while I was living in squalor. Happy squalor, but squalor nonetheless. For us to spend more time together, I needed to upgrade my accommodations. I rented an apartment located directly across from Cees's apartment. It was so close that we dragged a cable through the connecting windows to save on Internet charges. It felt more like a commune.

The house had been virtually abandoned by the owner, who had left for China. It was in a dismal state of disrepair. I did my best to shore it up for Rani's move, but it needed far more than a little fix-up. Because Amsterdam is built on a swamp, the houses are sinking year by year. What that means is that the interior of the houses twist and turn until they find a comfortable settling place against the wall of the neighbor's house. It's kind of like building a house of cards, with each card resting on the others to support the structure.

There were cracks all throughout the house, some small and others quite large. One in the kitchen was so large that it protruded a few inches from the wall. There was no chance to repair it, because even touching it would risk bringing the entire wall down. I didn't expect to stay in the house very long, so I left it alone.

One Saturday afternoon, Rani and I were making soup in the kitchen. Suddenly, we heard creaking and the next thing we knew, the wall was falling on us. I pushed Rani out of the way and tried to jump back before the wall came down completely. It landed on my shoulder and bruised me. Rani was okay and we had solved the problem with the wall: it was just gone. We spent the better part of the day filling trash bags with debris, over ten in all. I was told that we would be moving. Rani had had enough of my bohemian lifestyle.

This story typifies one of the reasons why I love Rani so much. Although she does not prefer to do or have something, she sees its importance to me and says we will allow it for a while. She does not deny what she would prefer, but she does not impose it. The same is true in return.

We have always had two major rules in our relationship. The first is that there is nothing we cannot speak about. And I do mean nothing—the entire book is open. And second, we will never dismiss a conversation. No matter how uncomfortable, it is not allowed to linger. We can always delay, but not dismiss.

One Friday night I picked Rani up from Central Station on my moped. I immediately saw that something was wrong. She was disconnected and not present. When I asked about it, she simply replied, "I don't want to talk about it."

I saw that whatever had happened still dominated her thinking, and she was suppressing the emotion behind it. I knew that if we didn't speak about it, it would consume our weekend. I asked again if she would be willing to share.

She adamantly stated, "I do not want to talk about it."

In what may seem to be lacking compassion, I said, "Then I guess I'll take you back to the station. There's no reason why both of us should suffer all weekend."

She burst into tears. I stopped the moped, turned the motor off, and hugged her. We stood on the street hugging for twenty minutes. We never spoke about what happened to her. It was no longer needed. She had let go of the emotion, and we were once again together.

With Rani, the point has never been to win arguments, but rather to see and be seen. Because of this, I have come to love her more and more over time. This is quite the opposite from every other relationship I've had, with a high energy in the beginning and then a gradual waning as I suppressed emotions over time. In Rani, I found something I never really believed in: my soulmate.

Now, in addition to my mentoring with Cees, I was growing on another front. Ten years after meeting her to the day (Christmas Eve), I asked her to marry me.

## CHAPTER 30

# SHEDDING MY
# SELF-IDENTITY

Although I went to Cees to learn, I was a stubborn learner. I loved learning, but I was protective of certain areas. I was comfortable with discomfort, up to a point. After that point I would shut down. Cees was very aware of that point and he would point it out regularly. The hard thing for me was that I had been shutting down for so long that I was no longer aware I was doing it, or how it was happening in me.

Cees was mostly patient with me, but there were a few critical moments when he held a mirror to my face in such a way that I had no other possibility but to look. One day, about five years into working with Cees, I said something that triggered him. Often, when I spoke about something, Cees could tell that I had no real awareness of the subject I was speaking about which was usually a memory, not a personal insight from experience.

He used this opportunity to do what many people might think mean. He began to chastise me with a venom that one would reserve for only the most hated person. He broke down my life and pointed out my hypocrisy and all of my behavior which was not genuine. He told me that people talked behind my back about how disingenuous I was. He left no stone unturned in destroying any idea I had of myself.

Some of the things he said included, "Andy, you often pretend you know more than you do—and everyone sees it. You act friendly, but you aren't really genuine. Everyone talks about you as being superficial. You are putting up a show and everyone sees through it. You are not delivering value in our partnership."

I was beyond distraught. The person I wanted to share my life's energy with was rejecting me and casting hateful words upon me. The entire experience was so overwhelming it made me physically ill, as if my body was realigning with this new reality. I crawled into bed with all of the symptoms of the flu. I sweated through my blankets and did not get up for three days. I did not eat and drank very little.

It felt like parts of my persona were sweating out of me and dying off. A sort of delirium came over me. I was losing touch with the person I had known as "Andy." Everything Cees told me were ideas I had of myself. I accepted them as true, and at the same time let them go. It was a full acceptance for Andy with all of his blemishes.

I mentioned how I experienced a sort of mental suicide after my mother's death. The difference between then and now was that my earlier experience was redefining who I was. This new process was about losing aspects of myself entirely. Accepting this loss was very much like experiencing death.

When I was young, I had been very insecure and needed the comfort of social acceptance. I went through the discomfort of my teenage years and finally found something I was better at than my peers: long jump. I found an identity that gave me confidence. In that confidence, I began to feel socially accepted. That all changed the day my mother died.

Later, I identified as a world traveler, then as a successful businessman. This all accumulated into a big sense of self-importance. Whether true or not, I had begun to think of myself as accomplished and important. In that identification, I became separate from myself and other people. By identifying myself as something, I began to again behave in that light. The effect was that people reacted to this identity. In turn, I was unable to move beyond problems I was facing in my own life. I was also unable to see what was right before my eyes.

To test this, I once asked a man I considered to be a friend how he felt about our relationship. We had worked together for almost ten years and I had become very fond of him. When I asked him, he looked almost shocked. He said, "I've never seen us as good friends." I realized that the person I saw myself to be did not match the experience of those with whom I interacted. This left a huge schism in my psyche. What could I believe anymore? More importantly, what had I been missing all of this time?

The only way I could begin answering those questions was by letting go of the picture of who I was. This process has continued ever since. Several of the biggest things I lost along the way included: the idea that I was great in business; the idea that I was easy to work with; the idea that my ideas were good; the idea that I really understood what people were trying to say. All of these things were no longer bundled up into the idea of "Andy," so something brand new began to emerge.

I came out of the three days in bed feeling completely different. When I saw Cees I gave him a big hug. He had given me a gift I could not imagine. Explaining this to others has been a challenge because it's hard to understand why one would be so grateful for what would appear to be such a vicious act. Yet because of what he had done, I was able to break a large part of the identity that I had not yet let go of—the Andy who, in spite of all his development, still wanted something outside of himself. To be liked. To be open. To be seen as special. With his biting words, Cees took away much of my lingering identity.

At the same time, I experienced something else that was quite curious. Although I had been unaware of it, prior to this experience with Cees there was a constant humming sound in my head. When I was a child we lived next to one of the world's most travelled freeways, California's 405. The sound from the freeway was constant—so constant, in fact, that after a time I associated the noise with silence. Similarly, a sound in my head was deeply connected with anxiety, which would anticipate all that could go wrong and plan to make sure it didn't happen.

This noise was something I recognized from back in my childhood. A flash came to me and I saw myself, as a child, anxiously walking up the stairs. I saw that the noise was my protection, a way to stay hyper-vigilant to the possibility that my father might explode at any moment. At the same time, I recognized that this noise had made me successful in certain areas of my life. For instance, when it came to management, I was quite good because I was able to anticipate all that might go wrong and course-correct quickly.

I had been doing that since I was younger than ten years old. Additionally, I had learned how to become acutely aware of people's emotions, which was a natural result of observing my father's emotions and anticipating his mood swings. In some strange way, my father's dysfunction had created a skillset I would use the rest of my life.

When I recovered from my experience with Cees, the noise was gone. There was no humming in my brain churning out thoughts. There was just pure silence. I began to hear the little voice inside my head clearly. The voice was soft and loving. It quietly observed the world in amazement. The loud version of myself would still show up and the voice would laugh at it, saying things like, "What are you trying to prove? What makes your thoughts so important? Why aren't you listening?"

All of the sudden, life felt so obvious, so clear. The peace I had found in the mountains of Annapurna was now possible in the middle of the tension of the boardroom. I was able to give space to the inner voice, regardless of where I found myself. I was feeling a deep connection with everything.

We are all here, brought together by some celestial act. We learn to adapt to our genes, upbringing, and social structures around us to become something. That something is always a mixture of what we decide within the confines of our surroundings.

Sometimes the surroundings are outside of us and sometimes inside. More often than not, it's both.

The higher we raise our consciousness, the freer we are to redefine ourselves and thereby everything around us. We are full of potential, but that does not mean that potential is always available to us. It is like a dormant volcano. It can explode at any moment. The explosion comes from deep within. The consequences can be felt miles and miles away. I saw all the dormant volcanoes, some trying to explode and failing, and some not even realizing they were volcanoes. My volcano had exploded. My world would never be the same.

The longer I worked with Cees, the more the stranglehold of my identity slowly lost its grip. Up to that moment, I had been many things: an athlete, a traveler, a businessman, and now a student of, and assistant to, someone who was trying to change the world. What I saw was that whatever idea I had of myself could change in an instant.

This left me with the question, "Who am I, really?" If I met the person I had been ten years earlier, I couldn't say I would actually like him. Who I am has evolved. When I look back at each person I have been, I realize those were just things I had been attached to, different people I aspired to be, different ways I wanted to be seen. Now I have less and less of a desire to be seen *as something* and more and more of a desire to just be seen.

Cees would often sing a song by a '70s singer Charlene. It's about a woman who wants to trade in her jet-setting lifestyle. She sings about various hedonistic episodes in her life, concluding that while she's "been to paradise," she has failed to find self-fulfillment, and expressed that in the line, "I've never been to me."

Up until this moment in my life, I felt very much like the Charlene song. I had spent years traveling from paradise to paradise, one exotic experience after another, but I'd never been to me. I had never seen that the beauty of life was always inside. I'd been too busy running away from it, not realizing that the pain was in fact the paradise. Living the sadness and allowing it to be embraced was counter to anything I would have ever imagined. But it was true.

When I look back at the most beautiful moments of my life, they are not the places I've been or the achievements I've enjoyed, but the sharing of intimacy. This was true on the farm in Australia, the little town in Japan, and on the streets of India. Beautiful moments have been times when I shared parts of me that I was afraid to let be seen for fear that I might be judged or rejected. For years, those fears guided me not to take risks for fear of failure. Now I see that the idea of failure was the grand illusion. As soon as I allowed myself to try, I succeeded, regardless of the actual outcome. Success is nothing but a continuing effort to aspire to be something greater than myself, to love and be loved.

Today, the man Andy is someone I like. He is honest and vulnerable and true to the challenge he is facing. He is not looking to start trouble, but he often finds himself there, because of his freedom to speak openly. In spite of this, he is loved. He is loved for who he is and how he has decided to express himself in the world. Instead of trying to be something, he has taken the risk to show up as he is, and allow the world to decide what to do with him. The road has not always been easy, but with every stumble he got up and kept walking. He always knew there was no end to the race, just a continual process of learning along the way.

As I look back at the shedding of all of my prior identities, I feel a deep sense of peace. I see that the ultimate shedding of my identity will be the actual shell that I call my body. When I finally have no more use for this, all the self-identity will dissolve—the ultimate release of whatever Andy was. He will return back to the particles he came from. I feel a peace in knowing that my journey is getting closer and closer to "me," in whatever shape and form that takes.

I cherish all the people who have shined a light for me. For many years, the tunnel was dark and at times it was almost impossible to find the exit. In one of life's great ironies, I needed to let go of life to once again begin living it and loving it. Whoever I may or may not be is no longer the question. The questions are, "Who am I now? What am I feeling? What am I avoiding? What opportunity do I have to use that energy to touch someone else and make life meaningful?"

I have found that the answer to this last question starts with accepting people unconditionally, just as they are, without any desire to "fix" or change them. It was in my relationship with Rani that I saw exactly what this meant in reality.

## CHAPTER 31

# LEARNING TO LOVE AND ACCEPT UNCONDITIONALLY

One of the challenges Rani and I had to overcome early in our relationship was what I call the "If you would only change" period. I was deep into my Meaningful Relations trainings and deepening my own awareness. Rani, on the other hand, was less focused on her emotional development. She loved to listen to TED talks, but I often saw it as an exercise to validate ideas she already had of the world. I was looking inward and seeing a world of wonder that felt never-ending.

I would often ask Rani to join trainings Cees and I gave on the weekends. She would respond, "It's not how I want to spend my weekend. It doesn't interest me." I thought she would come around in time. Yet that time never came. I began feeling tension inside as I observed issues developing in her life that could be resolved with some simple personal development work. But she was still not interested.

After a few years, I began to develop judgment toward her lack of determination to solve these issues. It was a pattern I recognized in myself from the past. I even saw it in the relationship with my father to me. When I cared about someone, I would get angry at that person for not doing what I felt was best for him or her.

This all came to a head one Saturday. Rani shared her frustration that she was being pushed into something she didn't want. I shared my frustration that she didn't try to deal with the emotional issues that had been impacting her for so many years. The conversation slowly moved from what our frustrations were with one another, to the things that made us frustrated to begin with. I shared that I felt we were growing apart. The further I went in my path of development, the more I felt we were moving apart. She shared that, although she was happy with my development, it was not her path. She just wanted to be accepted for who she was and not told everything she could be doing better.

I ended up breaking through this moment with the simple act of acceptance. I realized, "If I cannot love you for everything you are now, without needing you to be something else, then I cannot be with you. I need to love you for who you are and not what I want you to be."

With my simple act of acceptance, our lives changed. I was no longer agitated when I saw Rani suffering. In fact, I began to find it amusing. I realized that she apparently needed to suffer for some time before deciding to take action. For years, although I was trying to help, I had just been getting in the way. I am certainly not happy that she suffers, but I see that this is not my journey. It's not my problem to solve. And to love without expectation is something magical. It is a pure love that warms you up. It's not dependent on the other. It just says, "I'm here for you when you need me. I love you for everything you are, and whatever I think may be better is just my issue."

Since then, our relationship has grown stronger and stronger. A few years ago, I found her rummaging through her jewelry, as she often does, like a collector admiring her years of accumulating. Each piece holds memories for her. This time, one of the pieces caught my eye: my mother's wedding ring. It was the only thing I owned that belonged to my mother. After her death, I picked it out from the remaining pieces my brothers and I still had not distributed between us.

A sadness came over me. Tears welled up in my eyes. After so many years of running away from my mother's death, it was as if it all made sense. Here was a woman I loved as much as my mother, and she was holding the one thing from my mother that meant anything to me. My father had given her that ring over sixty years ago. It symbolized the love of two people who created me, which I never cherished because I only got to experience their breakup.

As Rani sat there holding the ring, I understood how beautiful it was and how beautiful my life was. I did not tell Rani then, but that was the moment I decided to ask her to marry me. For many this would seem like a normal progression, but for me this was something extraordinary. I viewed marriage as an arbitrary union that gave the government more control over my life. My friends often laughed at me as I would say, "I pay taxes, and the government already has enough control over me. As soon as I marry, I give them the right to dictate more."

In this moment, I decided that my mother's ring would adorn the one person who had come to symbolize that love now. I saw a beauty in that sadness that I cannot give words to. It was pure love. I spent the next weeks waiting for the moment which had been set in motion ten years earlier.

It came when we took off for a long weekend in London. It had been ten years to the day since we had first met. We spent some time sightseeing in London, where we walked 25,000 steps, as noted by Rani who is very precise in such matters. We were staying at a bed and breakfast in the Olympia District. I asked her to join me on a large sofa. She sat across from me with her feet draped over my legs. I had hidden the ring under a pillow, which she moved as she came to sit. I held the pillow down firmly so as not to give away the surprise.

I said, "Rani, it has been exactly ten years since we met."

She smiled and laughed, "Yes, I know."

I leaned over and said, "I want to ask you something."

She was intrigued but clearly not expecting anything out of the ordinary.

Then I asked, "Rani, will you marry me?"

Her eyes shot open as if she had taken a bite out of a lemon. She said, "No, you're kidding."

I said, "No, I'm not." I pulled the ring out from under the pillow where she was resting her leg. I said again, "Will you marry me?"

Her face turned soft and she began to cry. She said, "Yes."

A few months later, and about three months before our marriage, Rani came home and told me she had had enough of working in the Netherlands. She wanted to swim in a bigger pond: London. Although I had many reasons to stay in Amsterdam for my work, I saw this was her time to spread her wings and fly. Neither of us wanted to limit the dreams of the other. So when she asked if we could move, I took a deep breath and said, "Of course." Then I thought of the hundred things I would need to change in my life to make it work.

This ebb and flow of love and support has changed my life. It is this type of love that is difficult to give words to. Simply saying "I love you" feels so limiting. The love I share with Rani is the type of love that feels like life has purpose. Because I do not have children, I'm often told, "There are things you will never understand without having kids." I feel the same about my relationship with and love for Rani: there are things you will never understand until you have loved someone so unconditionally that it gives life new meaning.

It was in this love that I rediscovered the loss of my mother. It had been twenty-nine years since she died and I felt a complex mix of emotions. It was as if the sadness had become stale. It was not processed, but it felt so far away that bringing up the emotions did not feel genuine. It was as if I was watching a movie instead of experiencing my own life.

With this love, the memory of my mother's love became present. I remember discovering how it felt to be loved unconditionally, to be supported without reserve, to want to give to the other, just to feel the joy in it. In this love and support, I was once again able to allow the well of sadness to flow that had never been released from my mother's death.

My grieving came to a head in a session with a Core Energetics practitioner who helps people heal and transform, JoAnn Lovascio. During this session, I lay on the floor and she placed her hands on different parts of my body, asking me to speak and make noise. I followed along, but I felt myself distracted by her instructions. I asked her if I could say the things that were hardest for me to say.

She said, "Yes, please," as if welcoming the opportunity to make her life easier.

While lying there on the floor as she held me, I said, "Why don't you see me? Can't you see I'm suffering? Help me." All of the feelings from my eighteen-year-old self came gushing out. I was deeply connected to the wounds that had built up so much scar tissue that it felt almost impossible to massage it out. I cried and cried.

As I spoke, I saw that the pain was held in my throat, just as it had been with every prior emotional experience that was too much for me to bear. At one point it was so tight that I could barely utter a word. There were faint noises coming through the breath. Finally, I experienced a release of epic proportions. I embraced emotions that I had withheld for thirty-five years. It was magic. Everything that was shut down was now opening. I was not rationalizing the pain, I was feeling it. It was incredibly hard, but indescribably beautiful.

After the session, I felt alive. I sensed a deep connection to myself and the world around me. It was as if the pain was no longer a memory, but rather an old friend who was making a visit. To reduce this experience down to any single person or action would be too simple. This was the accumulation of everyone who had come into my life. Each person had taught me a lesson. Each person had given me tools to escape the emotional prison where I was held hostage.

I am indebted to all those people I've known and all those yet to come. The opportunity to allow others to influence you, and to influence others yourself, is a wondrous dance through life. The music changes and each partner has different moves to learn. I have been lucky to have danced. And I continue to dance. There are always new steps to learn. I am lucky because I now I have a partner with whom I can dance for the rest of my life.

Rani and I married on June 11, 2017. We chose the date because we both share it as our birthday. We wanted to surprise our friends, so we invited everyone to a "birthday party" for the two of us. Rani was turning forty and I was turning forty-seven. In order to keep up the appearance that it was an extra-special party, we told everyone the theme was "87 Shades of Red," adding up both of our birthdays. They had no idea they were actually showing up to a wedding. We celebrated and danced, symbolic of the meaningful moments we shared.

I understood that life needed to be celebrated. I could plan a party. Loss, on the other hand, was something that always showed up uninvited through the years. And there was more of it to come for me.

## CHAPTER 32

# SEEING MY FATHER

**W**hile working with Cees, I had one last chance to see my father. Rani and I went to New York to meet him for our favorite pastime: musical hopping. The three of us saw several shows and spent a lot of time together. I had an intuition that this would be the last time my father and I would be together. There were no specific clues, other than that he was looking frail and I did not see a fire in his belly to live. As our trip ended, we drove him to the airport and I walked him to the security checkpoint. I looked him in the eyes and, with tears streaming down my face, said, "I love you." I held him for some time, wanting to cherish the moment and remember him in my arms. I knew I would eventually lose him, but I had this moment now and I was not going to let it pass. I cried as I watched him walk away until he disappeared.

A few months later, I received a call from my brother. He told me that the bulk of the money my father had saved for us was lost in an instant. Millions of dollars were gone. When I was a child, my father had found an investment that brought a constant annual return of 15 percent. He was very proud of his ability to grow money, and his identity was very much attached to wealth, along with his ability to generate wealth for his clients. He had created separate investment accounts for each of us kids.

As a child I was always aware of this mysterious account, but I knew very little about it. Knowing the money was there always brought me great comfort, but I never took any money from it. It was now 2008 and the finance industry was reeling with the collapse of Lehman Brothers. The money my father had invested into this mysterious account for me had grown from a meager investment to close to $300,000. Additionally, my father had placed most of his personal wealth into the same investment, which allowed him to retire early and live from the dividends. He had lost a total of about $4 million, which included the accounts for me and my brothers.

As it turned out, this investment was part of the Bernie Madoff ponzi scheme. I was amazed by how little reaction I felt to this news. My immediate feeling was gratitude. I thought to myself, "If I hadn't known I had this money to fall back on had something gone wrong, would I have been willing to take all the risks in my life?"

Rani was astonished by my reaction and kept asking me, "Aren't you mad?"

I just smiled and said, "Look at what that money made possible in my life—without me even needing to use it."

I realized in that moment that money defines us based on our relationship with it. If we are scared we will lose it, we hold onto it and hope nothing bad will happen. If we see it as a means to happiness, we spend it quickly in order to get a quick high. In my life, money had always been simply a resource. If it existed, something was possible. If it did not, something was not. Giving it any more value added confusion to my brain. When all of the money was lost, I lost nothing more than a number on a piece of paper.

Unfortunately, this was not the case for my father. Following the collapse of Madoff, he was forced to not only reconcile the millions of dollars he had lost, but also the identity he had embraced for so much of his life: "I am good with money. I am wealthy." He had always felt like he had something to prove. He would often recount how many times his parents told him he would amount to nothing. So money was his way of telling the world he had made it, that he was someone to be respected. Now that the money had disappeared, he was going to have to reconcile this new reality and redefine himself.

This was incredibly stressful for him. He was devastated at disappointing his sons, and was unable to sleep. Forty-four days after hearing about the loss of the money, he called me and my brothers. He was going bowling that day and he simply wanted to say, "I love you." It was a short call. He gave no indication that it would be the last, but I believe he somehow knew, because he'd never called all of us on the same day.

After finishing his best game of bowling ever, he died of a heart attack. His last words were to make sure to take care of his dog, Molly, who was in his car.

My brother called me at 3 a.m., about six hours after we had spoken with our father. He simply said, "Dad died."

I lay in bed feeling numb. I've noticed that, when confronted with overwhelming emotions, my brain feels as if it is full of fog. I sat emotionless and told Rani the news. She began to cry immediately. It was only then that I could begin to grieve. It was in her pain that I could see my own.

Four hours later, I was on a plane from Amsterdam to Monterey Bay, where my father had lived. It was an incredibly beautiful time for me. I felt intense sadness and gratitude that I was able to sit with the deep love for my father. All my emotions were heightened. It was the first time in my life, since shedding so much of my previous emotional resistance, that I began to sit with the feelings of pain and celebrate them, instead of moving away from them. Each tear was a reminder of my genuine love for my father. Each tear, every moment of sadness, reminded me of how far our relationship had come.

When I shared with people that things with my father were

very good at the time of his death, they would often say, "Great, you found the opportunity to forgive him." I felt the same emotional reaction in myself every time. I hadn't forgiven him. I had finally seen him for who he was—someone who loved me but didn't know how to show it. I never had anything to forgive him for, because he had never done anything wrong to me. He had simply been reacting to his own pain and confusion in the only way he knew how. It just took me a while to figure that out.

As I had with my mother, I wrote a speech for him. This time, however, I also delivered it myself. I realized that, even if I cried in front of the audience, it was okay. That was who I was and how I was feeling. So I cried and cried and felt the release.

Many of his friends in Monterey were unaware of his emotionally challenging background. So they were surprised by some of the things I wrote. Unlike in the eulogy I had written for my mom, I did not try to sanitize his life. I shared that he was flawed and tortured. And most importantly, he was loved. I shared that the worst thing that could happen is that he would care about you, because it was in his incapacity to help that he became most violent. He was incapable of allowing helplessness and vulnerability to guide him. Instead, rage would often take its place.

When my father died, he was my close friend. I trusted and loved him. Given that I had spent so many years hating him, it is incredible to think this occurred. Although he changed a bit in those years, I changed a lot. I finally saw that I couldn't blame him for my pain. My life was not a byproduct of anything he said or did to me as a child. He was just a man, incapable in his own ways and yet full of love. As soon as I could accept that love in myself, I could begin seeing it in others, no matter how hard they might try to hide it on the exterior.

Only after I had learned to truly love myself and who I had become, could I begin to love him for who he was—not the man I once imagined I wanted him to be. He was in desperate need of the affection his parents could not give him. I found the beauty in my heart to see that we shared the same pain, the same human desire for love and connection.

## CHAPTER 33

# ANOTHER PROFOUND LOSS

After my father's funeral, I returned to Amsterdam to continue my work with Cees. Our lives both took a dramatic shift when Cees's cancer returned. He was scratching under his throat for weeks, picking at what appeared to be a ball under his chin. He did it so long that we could not tell if it was cancer or just the byproduct of him touching it so long. He told me he was certain it was cancer. It had all of the qualities of the last bulb that had shown up there.

He went to the clinic and the results were negative. No cancer. But Cees felt no peace. He was quite certain that although the results had been negative, they must be incorrect. After a month he went back to the clinic and asked them to rerun the tests. This time they did come back positive. Cees was not surprised nor in panic. It was as he expected.

From that moment, our lives changed. We did not think about how to create a business. We focused on how Cees wanted to live the last years of his life, regardless of what that meant. In the proceeding weeks we learned that Cees's cancer was a slow-growing form, which meant it was almost impossible to treat. The doctor told him there were no treatments available for his type of cancer. But on the positive side, it grows so slowly that he would have at least five years to live. Little did any of us know that Cees would live for less than a year.

Ever since my mother's death, I had stopped looking at time as something I could rely on. As soon as I knew I would be losing Cees, I did two things. First, I accepted his inevitable death. In that sense, I did not rely on him for anything in my work that would tax his energy. And second, I decided to take him on a trip.

After ten years together, he and I had not spent much time together outside of our work. We loved each other but we had so little in common that our conversations would often fall flat. I told him that I wanted to take a trip with him through the US, just him and me. It was June and I worked out a plan to drive from Colorado to San Francisco, hitting all the national parks along the way. On our flight to Colorado, the plane decompressed and took a dramatic nose dive to a safe altitude. As we sat, nose pointed down, I looked over to Cees and said, "This sucks. I'm going to lose more years than you." We both laughed.

When we finally landed safely and went to the car rental company, we were given a free upgrade to an extremely fast car: a Dodge Challenger with some special HEMI fuel injection. I did not tell Cees about the upgrade and walked to the cheapest car I could find on the lot. I put the key in the door, waiting to see his face as he would wonder, "How are we going to get halfway across the US in *that*?" After a few seconds, I turned and walked to the actual car. His eyes lit up like a child who had just been given a puppy. He loved fast cars and was over the moon. I got a picture of him leaning on the car in a dramatic pose, and we were off.

We drove for the next three weeks. We went through the beautiful Colorado mountains to the beautiful parks of Utah and

Arizona, finally making it to San Francisco. As we stopped at each site, we quietly took in the incredible beauty. At one point we drove up to the top of a cliff called "Dead Horse Point" and I took a picture of Cees as he sat looking over the cliff's edge. It was one of the last pictures I would take of him.

Along the way, Cees was very frail. He could only stay in the car for a few hours a day before he began to tire. He would often sleep and stare out the window. He'd apologize for not being able to keep me company as I drove. Our days were filled with vast silence. Often, hours would go by and we would just sit with no need for words.

The one exception to this was Dutch football. The World Cup just happened to be playing during our trip. Cees had to be in front of a television to watch the Dutch matches. This was not negotiable. On one day, the Dutch were playing Spain. They needed a win to advance to the finals. I had the bright idea to drive up the Pacific Coast Highway 1 on that day and find a bar where we could stop. I had no such luck.

What I didn't know is that there is very little to be found on the 1 between the Los Angeles area and Santa Barbara. Of course, the radio was on but sometimes it would go in and out as we drove along the coast. I was speeding to find a TV and thinking to myself, "How about this wonderful view to our left?" We finally drove inland about thirty minutes to find a small bar we found on Google Maps. When we arrived, we found out that the Dutch had scored five goals and the game was already over. Although his team had won, Cees was disturbed the rest of the day. He hadn't been able to share in the excitement of the moment.

But we had some incredible moments. I would wake up early and make him a vegetable drink that he had researched was good for cancer treatment. I would have the same. One time he said, "You know, I have never thanked you for how good you have been to me through the years. You have taken care of me and I have never told you how much I've appreciated it." We both cried.

Cees had two requests for the trip: He wanted to see whales, and he wanted to fly in a helicopter over the Grand Canyon. We were able to satisfy his first wish in Monterey, California. I had to say no to his second wish. His exhaustion had reached a point that I was afraid to add the eight-hour drive that was required to get him there and back. I still think about that today and have moments when I wish I had made the detour. Then I smile and think to myself that a helicopter ride pales in comparison to the trip he is currently on.

We had an incredible time together. We were simply together, without any drive toward the future. We were just two old friends enjoying the view. The trip was also a beautiful way to take in what we had achieved together. Although we never had an incredible financial success, we achieved something even more incredible: a life dedicated to something greater than ourselves, a purpose to share the beauty of life with the world. At the best of times, our work was a struggle. At the worst times, it was thoroughly exhausting. Yet we knew what we were doing and why: to move closer to the edge that makes life worth living. To feel that every day on this planet means something.

We eventually made our way back to Amsterdam. Cees was in incredibly good spirits because our trip had given him an awareness of what he had not yet shared with all the people dearest to him. He then called his closest circle of friends to thank them for being themselves. I heard him say over and over again, "I've been so busy telling you all of the things that you could improve on that I did not tell you how beautiful you already are. I'm sorry I missed it all of these years." I saw a love in him I had never seen before.

He and I had our last goodbye on the street in front of his home on the canal. Cees had purchased the ultimate camper van (created for a trade show) to demonstrate how far a camper van could live off the grid. There were so many buttons and gizmos that neither of us knew how to work it. After our trip together, he drove to Sweden in the van with his wife, Kai. It was there, on August 5, 2014, that he died. He had a heart attack sometime in the early morning.

Kai called me and screamed through the phone, "Cees is dead! Cees is dead!"

When I heard the news, I lay in bed, paralyzed. It was not all that dissimilar to the feeling of losing my mother. The wind had been knocked out of me. No matter how much I had prepared for that moment, it hit me as hard as if I had never imagined it. My friend was lost. Once again, death had taught me the value of life. We only have this moment before it is gone forever.

I spent the next week coordinating to get Cees's body returned to the Netherlands and help manage his funeral service. I managed the payments and logistics, but Cees's parents arranged the service. The funeral service was strange for me. The world that I had shared with Cees was not full of ceremony and formality. We had been all about intimate contact in intimate surroundings. The sterile environment of a funeral home was not the place I had imagined our last time together. I did not speak at the event. It was not what Cees and I had spent so many years creating: a space for vulnerability and love.

I took guidance from a dear friend, Joe, who suggested that I invite a few people from Cees's closest circle to come together and share in what we had called a "meaningful relation" session. About twenty of us gathered and we all sat in a circle in my bedroom. One by one, we shared what Cees had meant to us and how his life had changed ours. Several people shared that they would be divorced if not for Cees. Others shared the freedom they experienced in their lives. I shared that I had lost the man who taught me how to love again, the man who took me out of the hell I was living in and gave me the space to grow into my fullest potential.

There were tears. There was laughter. And there was great joy that we had the opportunity to have had him in our lives. To close, we played music and everyone danced. It began to rain lightly outside, which cooled down the warmth that had built up throughout the day. We moved outside to the garden and danced more. We celebrated a life that was beautiful. A life that brought life to others. A life that was now preserved in our memory.

My apartment in Japan.

Uematsu Sensei with a fellow teacher.

My intensive Japanese class in Tokyo.

One of the groups posing in front of
the sumo tournament banner.

Typical portraits of ancestors hanging in a Japanese home.

The Buddhist priest who took care of me.

The Buddhist temple where I studied religion in Japan.

Posing for a picture at the temple.

Newspaper clipping from Shinjo newspaper.

Hideki and Maki giving me a gift at my going away party.

The Annapurna mountains.

Children following
me in Nepal.

Mother making tea
for me in Nepal.

Crossing the peak of the Annapurna circuit.

Posing for the typical holding the Taj picture.

Picture of Cees.

The famous picture of Cees standing in front of the muscle car.

One of the last pictures taken of Cees as
he looks over Dead Horse Point.

The infamous camper van that Cees took on his final journey.

The last time Rani and I spent time with my father in New York.

Our wedding day.

## CHAPTER 34

# FINDING MY PLACE IN THE WORLD

A week after Cees's death, I finished the last details of his will. I was slowly coming to grips with the fact that, once again, my life was going to be totally different. After so many years of changing locations and vocations, I was beginning to find joy in change and to look forward to it. It reminded me that with the uncertainty of life comes opportunity.

I saw that the non-dual, non-identity space that Cees would often hold so dear was not getting me excited. I did not feel inspired to carry this torch further without him. I now needed to rethink where I wanted to put my energy. I felt fear, but also excitement. I have to laugh at the twenty-four-year-old version of myself starting off in business and just excited to get a job, and to be paid to learn, to feel like life was just beginning. I often feel that today when setting out on a new journey.

The one thing that was clear to me was that, in elevating Cees, I had neglected my own talents. I think this often happens between mentor and mentee. There is a time when the mentee believes he has to become a mirror image of the teacher, and I was certainly prone to that. But what I was just beginning to realize was that I had never fully expressed myself with everything I had learned over my lifetime. I had not yet discovered who I was in the world, without the inhibitions of before. I was not even sure who I would be.

Thankfully, I was surrounded by incredibly supportive people who believed in me more than I believed in myself. The one thing I knew for certain was that I would stay true to what I had learned. I just didn't know how I was going to bring it to the world. The opportunity came in the form of a project that would change my life forever. I was asked to help restructure a company that was failing and needed guidance.

One Sunday evening I received a call from my friend, David. David and I have been close for thirty years. He often confides in me and tells me about his business challenges. He is the oldest son of a wealthy family that at one time owned a major league sports team. My brother was his first assistant, and occasionally I was given small chores to do for David. For example, I started by cleaning his car. My brother handed me a Q-Tip and told me that every millimeter of the car needed to be cleaned. I literally used the Q-Tip to clean small cracks and crevices, such as the air conditioning vents.

From our first interactions, David and I always had a deep love for each other. Not the kind of love that they write about in movies, but the kind of love when you meet a kindred spirit and you see yourself reflected back in their eyes, as if you are confronted with the challenge of loving yourself as much as you experience yourself being loved by them.

It was in David's eyes that I began to touch my own pain again. For years, I had been told that I was avoiding my pain, that I was not in touch with it, that I needed to be something I was wholly incapable of being. The pressure just added to my misery, as if I had an open wound and salt was being poured onto it. "Just feel your emotions," people would say. What I did not realize was that, in touching my own emotion, I needed to find someone who could sit with my pain, not just jump over the inconvenience of it, as if there was a goal in mind. Someone who could just be with me.

In David I found an emotional soul mate. We spent a lot of time together through joyous and challenging times, always reminding ourselves of how difficult it felt to be loved fully, without reserve. On one occasion I was looking at David, realizing that we had spent much time talking about things, rather than simply being with the other. I shared with him how much he meant to me and how our relationship had changed my life.

He did as he often does: acknowledged what I said without allowing it to affect him deeply. I told him that I would not allow that, at least not this time. I again looked at him in the eyes and repeated myself until I saw the words penetrate him like a burst of love that was waiting to explode into space. He finally relented and gave the "thank you" of recognition I was waiting for—the "thank you" we often skate around in public, for fear that we might touch a nerve. We both were in tears. Eventually those tears turned into hysterical laughter as we began to see the absurdity of avoiding this beautiful moment.

If Cees taught me how to open myself up to love, it was my contact with David that kicked in the door in and said, "Here I am. You can avoid accepting it, but I'm not going away." In this relationship I learned many important lessons: love is a state of being; love cannot be explained, nor measured; love makes everything make sense. In his simple act of being with me, David taught me once again how to love, starting with myself.

I use this love to gauge how I am engaging with life. I often ask myself, "Do I feel the love at this moment? Or am I lost in thought?" If I feel love, then I allow myself to fully be, and I accept that whatever is said has the best intentions. If I feel thoughts creep in, then I slow things down and acknowledge that I am sitting with uncertainty. It is in this uncertainty that I've found that things can evolve to places I could not have imagined beforehand. When I'm with a coaching client and I'm not sure how to proceed, one of the first questions I ask is, "What is the thing you are most frightened to say?" The uncertainty of not knowing what they'll say or where it will lead opens the door to vulnerability, which in turn leads to discovery.

David and I had been speaking for a year about one of the companies he had invested in. Previously, we had decided that, although I had skill in areas that could help his businesses, he did not want to mix business and friendship. I had seen, through the years, how many personal relationships had turned sour over money, so I understood his reservations. Yet, at this point in my life I had no longer placed a line between business and friendship. I saw that keeping the so-called "private life" away from the business was just a coping mechanism, a way of avoiding vulnerability. If people did not know anything of my private life, it would be easier to shut them out when things turn bad.

On this call, it was apparent I would be able to support his endeavor. We both agreed that I would leave the following morning to help him. What I didn't know then is that I would spend the next three months playing hot potato with a business I knew very little about. I'd be doing this in the US, a country I had left twenty-five years earlier, which was in many ways more foreign than many of the other countries I had worked in.

It was Monday when I entered the first meetings with a group of six men, all of whom were very concerned. The venture capital money was running out on Friday, and if they couldn't come up with a solution, they would all be held liable. The company had already burned through well over $10 million of David's money. I started slowly by just listening. I heard contradiction after contradiction, but resisted the urge to point anything out. It reminded me of how a system can become so confused from within that no one sees how confused they all are.

I had the feeling that I was in the "matrix" and apparently I was the only one who had taken the red pill. Everything they were saying was all from the head, all logic. But nothing made any sense. It was as if everyone was blind to the obvious. Fear, uncertainty, and doubt guided everything, but no one was in touch with those painful emotions. The one thing I had learned in my time away from business was that the biggest breakthroughs occur when we lean into pain. What I was just starting to learn was how I would apply this newfound awareness in my approach to business consulting.

Instead of chiming in with a conflicting opinion, I simply asked, "Given that there is nothing anyone has said that makes clear why we should remain open, why don't we just shut it down?" The question was not asked with judgment or any strong belief. Rather, it was more like you might ask someone to pass the salt at the dinner table. The room fell silent. Although it had been on everyone's mind, no one was ready to entertain the possibility that everything they had built would be washed away in a moment.

The conversation turned. It was as if they were now facing the first step of mourning. They started accepting that the idea in their heads was no longer going to become a reality. The dialogue shifted from everyone trying to make a point to reconciling with this new reality. We spent the next days deciding what, if any, structure would be able to support the company going forward. It was clear that if they were to remain open, the entire structure would need to change radically. On Friday, just four days after my arrival, one-third of the staff (fifteen people) were let go. The only other option was to close the entire company. I had left corporate business life ten years earlier and this was my entry back into it. Included in the fifteen departures were virtually all of the senior staff, including the CEO, and all of the middle management. The only upper management left over was the CFO.

I was now left with the daunting task of building something up from the ashes of a fire that had left misery in its wake. One of my first tasks would be the most humbling in my life. I learned that, for the past three years, the company had not sent out invoices for services rendered. If we were going to survive, we would need to reclaim some of these costs. I ended up sending out a total of over 100 invoices, some with amounts over $100,000. Since I knew this would blindside our unsuspecting clients, I knew I was in for a world of hurt.

For the next few weeks, I took call after call from angry clients who yelled at me. I could not blame them. We were days away from closing our doors, which would have meant they would have lost all the data in the system. I simply said, "This is now where we are and we invite you to continue with us, or throw us out. I won't blame you no matter what you choose." Surprisingly, many of the clients stayed and appreciated the openness. Of course, some left, but that was the price of trying to build up the next phase of the business.

The three months were overwhelming. I had spent the prior ten years believing that love and openness could solve all of the world's challenges. Here, I was confronted with the fact that love can speed things up, but business acumen is equally important, if not more so in many cases. In my current work, I often float somewhere along this pendulum between heart and head space. The businesses that only look at the numbers tend to ignore the obvious constraints, which are almost always people. On the other hand, the businesses that are only about heart space often miss the determination of getting things done, especially when things get difficult.

This balancing act is central to everything I do today. If I meet someone who is more "heady," then I do my best to make sure they see that I can identify with their reality, and then present emotions in the package of something tangible. Conversely, if I meet someone who operates more from the heart, I meet them in love and point to the structure that they often do their best to avoid. This yin-yang of existence is virtually always in tension the moment we decide to step out the door—especially in business.

Unfortunately, we ultimately were unable to salvage the business David had invested in. The best we could do was to improve the product, at which point we sold the business for a nominal amount. The experience crushed me emotionally. It brought me back to humility in the realization that you can't solve every problem. For so many years with Cees, I believed that heart connection is enough to do it, perhaps not an easy journey, but it will get you there. I now realized that heart connection can get you clarity, but clarity will most likely reveal things that need to change quickly, and it may not be the outcome you want or expect. In other words, just because you're good at heart connection doesn't guarantee that everything will work out exactly as you plan in a practical sense.

The experience helped me get so much better at my work because I saw the impersonal side of business. Sometimes, it's just better to close things down than to continue beating your head against a wall. Sometimes you have to let people go, as much as it hurts. What may be perceived as heartless is actually the most loving act, if you're really seeing things in light of the outcome you're trying to achieve.

After three months of working with David's business, I cried for a week. It felt like I had PTSD. One of the reasons it hurt so much was because I felt like I had let David down. He had been betrayed by so many people during his life, and I wanted to be the one who could save something for him when it seemed impossible. I had failed. Even now, I could cry about it. It hurts because he trusts and loves me so much, and he's experienced so much disappointment and heartache in his life. But through the experience, David did feel my love in the act of simply trying. We became even closer through our suffering.

The experience again put me in touch with all the inadequacy CEOs feel. It reminded me of how much resolve is required to succeed in any business. And it also got me in touch with the mindset of how we emotionally get in the way of making obvious decisions. Because of this experience, I was propelled into working with some well-known people in business. What I quickly learned is that, to one degree or another, many of them feel like frauds. They have few people in their lives they can turn to because they're afraid of being vulnerable and having it be used against them.

From all of these experiences, I have learned one of life's greatest lessons: It's not important that you know what to do. What's important is that you know how to deal with the moment when you don't know what to do. It may sound counterintuitive, but in my experience, great leaders see *not knowing* as the gateway to possibility. In that space, they start asking liberating questions like, "If we were free to do this without limitation, what would we do?" or "What would need to change for us to accomplish this?"

Where I see this process fail is when fear and doubt set in. As soon as a leader looks at what is impossible, the realm of possibilities is limited by their own imagination. When questions are driven less by fear and more by curiosity, wondrous things tend to occur. It's a space where ego falls away and things become clear. It is the space where there is less control over the content (e.g., "Who has a better idea?") and more comfort in the process (e.g., "How do we make this happen?"). The ability to trust that love and compassion can guide a group is a true gift that needs to be nurtured. Once it is implemented, people never want to go back to the way it was before.

## CHAPTER 35

# DISCOVERING MY GIFT

One thing was becoming clear in my new journey: I was not a typical business consultant. I did not have all the answers. I did not have some formulaic, guaranteed path to success. I just had two observant eyes and an open heart. My greatest value came simply from pointing things out and asking open-ended questions.

After leaving and now returning to business, I changed one fundamental aspect of my approach: I shared what I saw *without reserve or judgment*. If I sensed defensiveness, I shared it in the moment and asked, "Why?" If I sensed anxiety, I stopped everything until we figured out what was going on. In essence, I took the x-ray glasses that I had found after my mother's death and put them back on. But this time, I was no longer judging myself or others for the things I was seeing.

What happened because of this was quite remarkable. People are not often told everything they need to hear—especially those in leadership roles. They're usually just told the things that are non-threatening. Thus, they don't see the full picture, and are consequently unable to make the most informed decisions possible. Using my newfound freedom, sharing became a wondrous challenge that would bring incredible discoveries.

For example, I once sat with a well-known and powerful Silicon Valley guru. He was planning a meeting for the following day with another high-profile venture capitalist, for whom he had such admiration that he no longer saw him as a human being, as if this other person had some sort of superpower.

I laughed and said, "You're an idiot. How would you feel about me if I treated you with such high respect? Would you want to spend time with me? Why would you think this person would want to spend time with someone who treated him that way?"

Although I called him an idiot, it was in a lighthearted way so as to jolt him a bit with clarity. I pointed this out with love and compassion. I was potentially risking everything. But I really wasn't. I was with him because of my ability to speak with clarity and love.

As the point sank in, he smiled. An entirely different discussion then ensued. The questions turned to, "What do you still have to prove? Where have you not fully embraced your own capabilities?" These types of questions inevitably lead back to the heart of just about any challenge: an idea we have of ourselves that defines what is possible—and what is not. In this case it was a simple case of, "I still have something to prove."

When it comes to my work, instead of falling back on opinions and beliefs, I have allowed my "third eye" to be in the driver's seat for a while (the same "third eye" I became acquainted with in the temples of Japan and later the mountains of Annapurna). One might call it intuition. To me, it is the seat of consciousness— the observer of my thoughts, emotions, and experiences. It is a space of non-judgment. The third eye does not judge, interpret, evaluate, diagnose, or react. Rather, it simply observes reality as it is, in every moment. What it has shared throughout the years has shocked even me. If I feel my own emotions bleed in, then

I know my words are tainted with a part of Andy that is not yet at peace. I've been compassionate to that Andy, knowing he has room to grow.

I'm sure you've heard the saying, "Don't assume, or you'll make an 'ass' out of 'u' and 'me.'" This is where I spend probably 80 percent of my time in supporting others today. In the past, I've made so many decisions without fully understanding the assumptions upon which I based my decision. I've learned to analyze my assumptions because, when I understand the assumptions I'm operating from, my decisions are so much more conscious.

I think back on my experience of traveling through China and trying to order from the Chinese menus. My assumption was that, by pointing to an item and raising my index finger clearly communicated that I wanted one of that thing. I remember thinking to myself in frustration, "How can you possibly not understand that?" In my "obvious" logic, I failed to see the obvious assumption. The Chinese operate from different assumptions. Neither set of assumptions are better than the other. They simply are. But in order to navigate them, we first have to see them. This recurring story is critical to virtually every challenge we face and, unfortunately, it tends to get ignored.

If I look back at every problem I have ever encountered, it has always been a byproduct of my brain latching onto an assumption and then using it as a fact. As long as I'm unwilling to see that I have made that assumption, I am *always* part of the problem. Thinking that you know something while also being open to an entirely different understanding is one of life's greatest challenges. It is also the place where I find some of my greatest joy and fulfillment. It reminds me of a Buddhist monk who spends days drawing wonderful images in sand, then lovingly blows them away. I'm always asking myself, "How willing are you to blow your truths away? How willing are you to consider that the limit of your senses may mean you've assumed incorrectly all of these years?"

I see that my life is an accumulation of experiences. These experiences allow me to look to the past in order to predict the future. Of course, without this ability I would not have been able to adapt, learn and thrive. The one thing that sits like a rock in my shoe is the thought that everything I know is a memory. It is stored somewhere in my brain. And although the conditions may have changed throughout the years, I am continuously projecting this past onto the present. If I do this without awareness, then I am unwittingly creating the reality of the past over and over again, and assuming that it occurred independently of me—as if I had little to do with the outcome. I had blamed Gerhard at TOPCALL for being dishonest, and my father for being violent, when I myself was no different.

In my past thirty years, after living in seven countries, I have seen that much of our lives are defined by the cultures we're raised in. In Detroit, I saw that education was not an option for Tyrone. In Australia, I saw that the Bomford family's isolation excluded certain possibilities for them. In Japan, I saw Miyu, unable to follow her love of music because her family came first. And these were just the obvious things. The education and social environment for all those individuals were reinforcing a life of expectation and social obligation.

We often have ideas in our heads that we truly believe are based on our own thinking. But to what degree are we just following patterns passed down generation after generation? This process runs just fine until we turn these blind expectations into a reality that we then project onto others. Take, for instance, the moment you see yourself observing another's behavior and making assumptions about where it is coming from. You're believing that you have the ability to determine what is "right" and "wrong" behavior. This is what I did for many years after my father kicked me out of the house. I told the same story over and over again, in order to promote the story that I was the victim of a vicious father. That stopped the moment that I no longer focused on his actions and instead completely embraced his intentions.

Yet, it is hard to break the cycle of noise in the brain. In order to stop it, I had to see that I was no longer my thoughts. Whatever I see now as my reality is really just my brain taking shortcuts all the time. Things that I've seen thousands of times are labeled and not given further consideration. Everything new that I encounter is compared against everything I have experienced before, and this defines my context for experiencing reality. Interestingly, this "reality" is quite different for everyone, as any two people's memories of the same experience can differ tremendously.

Though predicting the future based on past experience has its advantages, it also causes us to miss out on our current experience. We create our reality, in large part, through the way we interact with it. Everyone we encounter on a daily basis is, in some way, reacting to us. Their behavior, therefore, is a consequence of our own actions. This is opposed to the story that people are always the same in every situation.

I began to enjoy the process of deconstructing everything down to its base reality (its "is-ness"), seeing it beyond the label or conceptualization it carries, or the category it has been placed in. Chairs, books, signs, trees: we learn the words and then we stop thinking about them. Our curiosity is gone. Yet the reality of what that thing really is, is beyond the label we assign to it.

In this deconstruction, my head relinquishes its need to control. It cannot grasp the object and relegate it to a category. In these moments, I allow my brain to sit free of constriction and direction. My job is to listen attentively to the process. In spiritual language, this is referred to as the constant listener, or the observer, the quiet observer of the dynamic between all the players speaking in your head.

To illustrate, take a moment and close your eyes. With your eyes closed, remain silent and observe your thoughts. Do not think, or try to create thought, but let it emerge naturally. Do not think about a thought once it arises. Just let the thought be there. You may notice your mind's desire to jump into a single thought. Avoid it, without blame or judgment.

What you may see is that the thought emerges from nowhere—which is quite amazing, when you consider it. You do not create thoughts. Rather, they emerge from the ether. On the bright side, you don't need to feel guilty about it. Yet this does not let you off the hook for what you do as a result of these thoughts. It just means you can accept that your thoughts are not under your control. You can take responsibility for where these thoughts lead you, and follow the voice that is purest of heart. The silent observer is your guide as you discover more about yourself and the world around you.

At the end of this book, I will ask you to blow away some of the assumptions you have made from the past. Like the Buddhist monk, you too will find that beauty is in the creation and not the possession. Your thoughts are also a beautiful picture. In many cases, you have spent years drawing them in your head, and there is a beauty in blowing them away.

## CHAPTER 36

# THE PARADOX OF
# MY WORK

C hange is hard. It is messy. It does not give us the control we desperately desirc. Yet it is a constant reality. In my work, I constantly struggle with knowing the best way to support people. More often than not, what they need is at odds with what they think they want. It reminds me of the Rolling Stones song, "You can't always get what you want. But if you try sometimes, you just might find, you get what you need."

This is where I see a balance between Eastern and Western philosophies. In the simplest terms, the East is primarily about feeling whole, while the West is primarily about achievement. I have seen that the strength of each side often limits the potential of the other.

For instance, I am working with the CEO of an IT company. It is a multi-million-dollar business that is expanding quickly. The CEO has an issue with phrasing anything in the negative form. "We are not making our numbers" is translated into "We have room to improve." "His behavior is a major problem" is translated into "There is space for him to grow." At face value, it would seem like rephrasing things like this in a more positive light is helpful.

But the challenge comes when, in order to move in a fundamentally different direction, you must first gather resolve that almost always comes in the shape of a clear "no." A "no" comes from a deep place in the belly that says, "From this moment forward it is going to be different." It is neither positive nor negative. It feels uncomfortable because it does not allow stagnation. It forces change. It is determination. Living a life of only positivism will often make it harder to connect with the "no" inside yourself.

To understand what happens when a person lives from only the positive, consider this example: A man lives in a house that gets flooded regularly. Whenever the floods come, he buys hundreds of bags of sand to shore up the outside of the house and keep the waters at bay. Year after year, he buys more bags, positively telling himself that if he just remains determined, he will overcome the ever-increasing water.

The problem is that the fundamental issue of rising water is never dealt with. The question is never asked, "What is the root problem, and what's a better way to go about addressing it?" Instead, we fall back on a belief, and it's usually one that we are not even aware of: "If I remain positive, it will bring me to a better place."

The truth is, challenges are neither positive nor negative— they just *are*. The very idea of positive and negative blocks us from dealing with reality as it is. When we operate from a space of value judgment (i.e. "good" or "bad"), we experience either stress or joy when dealing with challenges, depending on how things are going.

I was once working with a CEO who was frustrated with an employee. She said, "He is not doing his job."

I asked, "What is he not doing?"

Then the list of frustrations came out like a trial lawyer.

I asked, "What have you done about it so far?"

Another list of stories emerged, reinforcing the idea that there was nothing that could be done. What I heard was that the CEO had already decided that she did not want that employee and she was building a case to get rid of him. I asked, "Have you considered bringing these things forward to him in a way that he can see that there are consequences if he doesn't change?"

She resisted as she tried to convince herself that she had already done that. Then something magical happened. We had a three-way meeting. The CEO could no longer write the story because the employee was now sitting with us. Instead of behaving angrily, the CEO shared how difficult the situation was, and the position she would be in if it did not change. The employee was surprised. He had never realized the CEO was that dissatisfied.

By the end of the meeting, deep appreciation was felt on both sides. There was no longer an expectation existing only in the mind of the CEO, which had been an unfair projection onto the employee and only served to cause frustration. And the employee was now completely aware of what he needed to improve in order to thrive in the environment.

This all may sound obvious. My question is, why does it almost never happen this way?

The answer is quite simple: We are very often blind to our expectations, and we simply react to them! We do not let the silent observer in to have a look and see exactly what we are reacting to. Then we do the unthinkable: We operate from the space of "right" and "wrong." We engage the other person in a way that alienates him and does not serve our mutual interests.

When you see yourself coming from the space of value judgment (this is good, this is bad) and not observation (this is not getting done, this has consequences) you will see that you are creating unnecessary tension, and in many cases sabotaging your own success. What is the alternative? Observe, without interpretation. It changes everything! Instead of telling someone what she is doing wrong, simply make the observation, without judgment.

For instance, "In the last two months, I see that you have not been able to meet the deadlines we have set. What is the problem?"

In this space, we have plenty of room to explore what an alternative might look like. When we are not caught up in right or wrong, we're more likely to think creatively about potential solutions. We are more likely to leave the other person in a motivated state.

So, if all this is true, why do we continue to go through the world with such rigid ideas of right and wrong, good and bad, true and false? The answer to that question brings me back to a recurring theme. Who we identify ourselves to be defines us. We are the person who gets things done, we are the leader, we are powerful, we are wealthy, we are quirky, we are the rebel, we are difficult, we are smart, we are dumb, we are lazy. How can we see that we are more than the identity or label we are so comfortable with?

So, where does the "no" come in? Assume that you don't place a value judgment on "no"—it's not bad, it just is. It's an objective state that exists like any other. Now, it can play an amazing role. In the "no" is found an explosion of tension and creativity. If we say "no" to one thing, it places our mind in an almost immediate state of friction. If no, then what? Our mind tends to scramble to fill in the hole that is now left behind.

What if we do not force an immediate solution, but instead we allow for further exploration? Then we might even welcome the "no" as a means of inspiring creativity. The challenge is to hold back on devising solutions. It is in human nature to want to solve things. We are not trained to explore areas we're unfamiliar with. We tend to avoid those spaces. So in order to create meaningful change, it often begins with a "no" to the current situation we find ourselves in, and an openness to explore without jumping too quickly on any single solution.

## CHAPTER 37

# CASTING OFF CHAINS OF SELF-IDENTITY

If there is one thing I've learned on this incredible journey through life, it is that I am never truly certain of anything. For me, the starting point of learning to be comfortable with uncertainty was when I learned to see my self-identity for what it is: nothing more than thoughts and ideas I have in my mind about myself. Self-identity, like our beliefs and opinions, is just smoke and mirrors.

When I was an athlete, I had certain ideas about myself. When I was a traveler, I had other ideas about myself. And when I was a businessman I had yet other ideas about myself. It has always been my self-identity that determines my values and what judgments I make with those values. Those values have changed throughout the years, but they have always been tied to different versions of "Andy."

What happens when you no longer see yourself as just an identity? How does your perspective and behavior change when you begin to observe your identity and no longer assume that it is who you really are? When you do so, it is like you are looking at yourself as another person and saying, "His opinion is just as valid as anyone else's. And it should not be taken at face value."

Take any difficult situation with another person where you are currently stuck. See the value judgment you are placing upon it. Take a moment and think about it. What did the person do? How do you feel about it? Now, consider for a moment, what is the expectation you had? Now ask yourself where this expectation comes from. Stop trying to defend the expectation because it is an "obvious" expectation to have. That is just your identity speaking.

I was once helping a CEO with a small video project. A few weeks after the project, he came back to me asking for support with a website project. In his mind, he had established that however I helped with the video project, it would be the same with the website. Yet unlike the video project, the website required much more hands-on time, which I did not have available.

At some point this time issue came to a head. The CEO explained to me that he felt anger for some time, and was resentful that I did not fulfill my promise to support him. I was surprised. He had felt this way for many months and yet had not shared it with me. I was not even aware that his expectation was different than mine. He shared that he felt betrayed. As I was unaware of his expectations and they had not been expressed directly, it took this moment to find clarity. In the end, it was very clear that I was being judged for failing to meet unspoken expectations. We eventually found one another again, and our relationship has grown even stronger because of this encounter.

Consider how different your life would be if you no longer fell prey to blind expectation but instead, saw expectation as an opportunity to connect with people.

"I see that I wanted you to be here on time and I never made it clear that I would have to let you go if that did not change."

"I see that I never told you that I was uncomfortable when you work late which has meant that I am not always nice when you get home."

When we make judgments, we're not able to truly see ourselves, other people, or situations objectively. Take where you are at this moment. Look up at the corners of the room you are currently in. If you are outdoors, look for a tree or something above you. Now, while keeping yourself in this position, move your awareness to look down at yourself from above. If it doesn't come easily, give it some time. See yourself from the perspective of the one above you. See yourself move. Observe how you are positioned. Observe your movement. Hold this observation and let your mind float for a moment. The person you are now looking at is just another person in the world.

From this perspective, you will see things that surprise you. This process of observation is where confined identity begins to fall away. When I say "confined identity," I'm referring to the inability we sometimes have to alter our behavior because of ideas we have about ourselves. We take our "self" so seriously. From the observer in the corner of the room, we can have the person reading this text do whatever we want. They could suddenly shout at the top of their lungs. Or laugh out loud. We can ask the puppet to smile. In essence, we are free to be the puppeteer as well as the puppet.

We like to distinguish ourselves from animals with the idea that we have free will. Yet the vast majority of our actions are mere patterned reactions, conditioned behavior, just like animals. Just because our patterns may appear to be more complex than animal patterns doesn't mean they are all that different. The difference is that we are aware of our own identity, and therefore we can project ideas and beliefs onto ourselves, for instance, "I am smart," or "I am attractive."

Another option is to see that we are everything we define ourselves to be, but not all of them at the same time. Saying, for instance, "I am a human being," or "I am an organism," or "I am a bunch of particles" is one way of limiting this identification, and therefore creating less separation between ourselves and the world around us.

And yet, there is an irony in all of this. If I am so uncertain, then why do I feel the freedom to write this book with confidence? It is because I learned that I can trust my experience and at the same time embrace how limited it is. When I am in a discussion and someone says, "You do not understand," I light up. What do they see? What might I be missing? I treat my life like a big science experiment. I have a working assumption that I am excited to falsify. The alternative would be looking only to validate the things that I feel that I already know, which tends to create self-fulfilling prophecies. At that point, my experience would not necessarily add to my value. And in many cases, it would create limitations. Instead, because I take my experience seriously but hold it lightly, it acts as a north star.

As I've pondered over the years on this idea of self-identity, a fable came to me. I call it the "Fable of Jan, the Mirror Maker":

*Jan lived on a tiny street in the busy town of Amsterdam. He lived in a bright house with big windows that let light cascade in. He built mirrors for the royal families of Europe.*

*One day, while building his largest mirror yet, out of the corner of his eye he saw a reflection of the most beautiful woman he had ever seen. Entranced with the vision of her beauty, he stood paralyzed.*

*Suddenly, he awoke from his trance and ran outside to chase the woman who had captured his affection. He looked up and down the cobbled street. But she was gone. After hours of searching, he returned to his home. All he could think of was the beautiful woman.*

*For days, he stared out his window, hoping to catch another glimpse of her passing by. Weeks and months passed with no hint of the woman of his dreams. Jan fell into a deep depression.*

*One day, while gazing at his reflection in one of his mirrors, he fell apart. In a fit of rage, he smashed all his mirrors onto the ground, shattering them into thousands of pieces. Breathing heavily, he fell into the middle of the pile, staring at the mess. In the shards, he saw a faint image of the woman he was searching for. He scraped around and picked up shards of glass to build the face of the woman on the floor.*

*He became consumed with the project. He noticed that tinier pieces rendered better detail. So he kept breaking the mirrors into smaller and smaller pieces, bloodying his fingers with each detail. He added an edge here, an angle there. This continued for months. He lost weight, his job, and eventually his home.*

*Movers came to remove his belongings from the home. One of the men looked at the glass image on the floor and was stunned. He turned to Jan and said, "I know that woman."*

*Jan stared at him in disbelief. He begged the man for an introduction. He told the man that if he brought Jan to her, he would give him the last of his money.*

*The man agreed. That evening, Jan followed the mover to a quieter part of the city with large, ornate buildings. The man guided Jan inside one of the buildings, which was quiet and dimly lit. Jan carried a lantern low to the ground to make sure he didn't trip on anything as they made their way down a dark corridor. They arrived at the end of the corridor. The man raised his lantern high.*

*Jan looked up and saw the woman of his dreams staring down at him. But it was not a woman at all, but rather a painting with such fine detail that he had to look twice to be certain. He stood there in shock. With tears in his eyes he murmured, "An image."*

*The mover told him he had delivered the painting a year earlier and had passed by Jan's home on the way. He laughed and said, "You must have seen me pass with her then."*

*Jan realized his misfortune. He had lost everything, all for the love of an idea that had never been real.*

All of us spend our lives chasing images in the same way. These images are the concepts, ideas, beliefs, opinions, and judgments we have for ourselves and others. We argue and fight with each other over these images. At the extremes, we even kill each other over them. If you look at war and tension between people, you can often see their projection onto themselves (e.g., "I am Israeli," or "I am Palestinian"). Even nationality, which no one even chooses, is a projection. As soon as I've stated myself as something, I'm connected to an identity. I either gravitate to it or react to it.

But as Jan discovered, none of these images are real. They are only ideas in our head. They confine our perceptions and choices. For example, if I hold the idea, "I'm not a good writer," then that idea will hold me hostage and I will never try to write. If I believe I'm not smart, I may not go to college, thus cutting off thousands, maybe millions of potential options.

The more we hold onto an image of ourselves, even an image of who we don't want to be, the more we operate in the world blind to the consequences of our actions. In my experience, allowing certain ideas of myself to die has been a journey to an ever more fulfilling life. The more we understand and accept ourselves, the easier it is for us to be whatever the present situation requires.

Letting our self-concepts die is not easy. In fact, it is like mourning a death. Once we let a piece of ourselves go, then we are confronted with our mortality. If something I held so dear is no longer there, then what else might disappear as well? When people retire, they are faced with the challenge of re-creating meaning and purpose. They once got their identity from work. Another example is professional athletes who have a hard time transitioning into something else after their sports career.

*Learning how to allow parts of us to die before our actual death is one of the hardest journeys to take.* But when we take that journey, new areas of exploration, which we've been closed to in the past, open up to us. All the secrets we've carried, worrying about what people would think of us if they knew, are exposed.

Self-identity often discourages experimentation. Self-identity often arises as we feel pressure to conform to societal norms. The more we conform, the more our authenticity and creativity are stifled. What's left are fear and self-doubt. We hear platitudes like,

"You can be anything you want to be," or "The sky's the limit." But locked in the chains of self-identity, our minds shut down many possibilities. We work within the confines of creativity that have been predetermined by and for us.

My friends have two daughters. I once gave one of their daughters a toy as a gift, which had a predetermined scope of creativity. I saw discomfort in the mother's eyes when I gave it to her daughter. She thought that a "paint-by-the-numbers" approach was not creative, but rather logical. In a paint-by-the-numbers exercise, we give children a goal and a set frame in which their play occurs. I saw in this a larger application: How many things, which we have come to view as "creative," are nothing more than predetermined paint-by-the-numbers activities, passed down from one generation to the next?

Our entire society is permeated by an aversion toward experimentation and failure. Neither schools nor businesses reward failure—instead, they punish it. We don't value the fact that failure is a necessary part of learning and innovation.

So if we open our minds to the possibility of failing, how do we address the fear, insecurity and self-sabotage that arise in this process? It all comes down to one critical factor: self-acceptance— loving ourselves for who we are—without defining ourselves by it.

For example, I have deep insecurities about public speaking. When I plan to speak to a group from a position of authority, I feel all my nerves rise up. What I've learned to do is embrace that insecurity—love it as a part of me, and speak from that place. For me, preparing a speech is more about finding my center than it is about preparing what I'm actually going to say. If I feel myself incapable of sinking into myself, I see that everything I say is just a memory from the past, potentially without relevance to the people that I'm currently with. Those memories from the past are all part of the construct of self-identity, which constantly constrain our possibilities.

Once you've given up on the need to succeed in order to bolster your self-identity, it will no longer limit you. Before shedding my self-identity, I lived in constant comparison to an expectation of how I "should be." Afterward, I had no concept of failure. If I did, it was only that failure was not allowing myself to try. I no longer needed to achieve to feel a sense of peace.

I also no longer depended on social acceptance to validate my self-worth. Up until this point, I had always lived within the realm of social graces. I did my best to fit in, and that got me quite far. Anyone can go far with social skills. But the questions I couldn't answer satisfactorily were, "Has it been worth it? Has my time on this planet meant something?" I couldn't answer "yes" with any degree of confidence. And I often looked enviously at the people who rebel against social norms and define their own way in the world.

Wanting that for myself, the first thing I changed is that I took my own experience seriously. Before my "awakening," my modus operandi was to read tons of books as a way to arm myself with "knowledge" and gain a sense of self-importance. My thought was that, the more I knew, the more special I would be. I found, however, that the more I read that didn't connect with my own experience, the more I got lost in the thoughts and ideas of other people. I didn't truly "know"—instead, I was just spouting the experiences, beliefs, and opinions of others.

This realization drastically changed my life. One of the first things I noticed was a noise that was always running in the back of my head, like a whispering voice reminding me of all the anxieties I should have. This voice was so common that I forgot the possibility of a life without it. It was only by giving space to my senses that I began to hear the voice more clearly. I realized then that fear and its constant need for control and security had dominated the greater part of my life.

Now, as I have shed my self-identity, the voice is no longer distracted by reactive thoughts. I have noticed that in many cases, this voice was reacting to unrealistic fears from the past, and in other cases, real situations that were asking for attention. By allowing all the voices in, without passing judgment, I began to sense a deeper intuition that I was not using to its fullest potential.

I also stopped ignoring the emotions that feel like they're attempting to block me from moving forward. Now I don't resist them—I embrace them. These emotions are usually the function of some aspect of self-identity. In other words, if I allow myself to fully embrace, "I'm a bad public speaker, and it's okay," my fears settle. Conversely, allowing myself to see that, regardless of my ideas, I'm a fantastic public speaker means that I am free to simply be and not be determined by any idea I might have of myself. So, embracing these emotions has been one way to release layer after layer of the ideas I have about myself. And embracing them is, paradoxically, the process by which we allow them to dissolve.

I have often heard of this process called a loss of identity, to the point that you feel one with everything, with no separation between yourself and the world around you. I certainly cannot say I inhabit this space as a constant state. But I can say that when I'm not in it, I'm aware that I'm not. Searching for this miraculous space is something of a paradox. You don't find it, but rather it finds you.

So embrace, embrace, embrace. There are many techniques for doing this. Each method provides a perspective and a good place to start. However, any methods are just stepping stones into deeper insight. Once you learn the technique, you can give yourself the result that the technique allows you to find. Your dependence on the tool will drop away. Once you embody the core understanding, you are free to forge your own path, and tools are simply a means and not the way.

I am often asked more detailed questions about the "how." This book is more about my journey and less about the actual tools, yet there is one tool that I have used often. It was developed by Peter Koenig, a British man who spent years studying people's relationship with money. He teaches that money is nothing more than an idea projected onto pieces of paper. (Even that is not completely true, because less than 1 percent of the money that exists in the world is actually printed. It is a virtual number on digital screens.) Money only exists because of our collective projection. Everyone projects something different onto money. Therefore, each person's relationship with money is completely different.

Projections, whether conscious or not, always materialize in our lives. If you project onto money that it is a burden, then money becomes a burden for you. If you believe money provides freedom, then you won't be able to be free without it. The effects of projection can't be overstated.

The irony is that by projecting unconscious beliefs onto money, we create the opposite of what we really want. If I project security onto money, the result is that I chronically feel insecure. If I project happiness onto it, then I'm constantly unhappy as I chase money. If I believe money is a burden or confusing, I will constantly push it away.

To change our relationship with money, we have to uncover our unconscious projections. From there, we can reclaim the attributes we've projected onto money. We reclaim a part of ourselves which has not been allowed to be freely expressed. For example, if I project security onto money, that comes from something deep within me that has felt deeply insecure financially, most likely from childhood experiences. As long as I project security onto money, I can't heal that deep insecurity in myself. By owning the projection, I find the insecurity, which then gives me the ability to deal with it.

Consider the belief, "Money is power." First, we turn it around in order to analyze it. Essentially, this projection means, "I am powerless without money." Next, we reclaim the projection— we remove the focus on money to discover the incapacity or insecurity in ourselves. The projection has nothing to do with money. What it really means is that we feel powerless. Finally, once you own that insecurity, then you accept it as it is, without resistance. "I am powerless, and it's okay." Our deep wounds are healed only by the complete acceptance of them.

Carl Jung said, "Until you make the unconscious conscious, it will direct your life and you will call it fate." Identifying and dealing with our projections is one of the most powerful tools for personal growth because it makes the unconscious conscious. It allows us to see all the hidden ideas and beliefs that limit our freedom. Consciously identifying our unconscious projections opens up a whole new world of possibility. They can only hold us captive as long as we are unaware of then.

By continually reaffirming what is possible and true for you, nothing will change in your life. The only way to change your life is to reclaim your projections, which flow from your beliefs. And the only way to reclaim your projections is to accept yourself in all your incapability, insecurity, and vulnerability.

## CHAPTER 38

# HAPPINESS CAN'T BE FOUND

**B**eginning at the moment of my mother's death, I forgot happiness could exist. I had all but given up on it. I experienced distractions and moments of fun, but no real happiness.

In much of my work today, I am confronted with a strange paradox: People often come to me with the expectation that they will be happier afterwards. I always meet this expectation with some resistance, because happiness is not something I can promise. In fact, people may be left less happy after our interactions. I laugh often as I see that the ideas we have about happiness are often what inhibits us from experiencing it to begin with.

Looking again at projection, you will see that once you have predetermined what happiness is "supposed" to look like, you are a slave to that image in your head. So if you are unhappy because you're unmarried at thirty, or divorced at forty, or unemployed at fifty, these are simply expectations that you have blindly accepted as important to be happy. What if you did not have these expectations and you simply woke up, saw the sun and thought, "Wow, I've got another day to live!"

My experience with happiness is that it's not something you find. Rather, it finds you. This doesn't mean you're left helpless— far from it. Just like a marriage between two people, happiness needs work, except this happiness work is done on the relationship inside yourself. The emotional and rational aspects of our being are often at odds with one another, and it is not until we open up and start to move through this internal conflict, that we can begin to feel childlike joy again. When I was mourning the loss of my mother, I was unwilling to move into the tears that came with healing. I judged myself. I was unable to allow happiness into my life because, paradoxically, I was unable to allow sadness in.

Happiness arises when nothing prevents it from being there. So rather than it being an active process, it's more like a phenomenon that appears when it has no reason not to appear.

There's a difference between short-term experiences that create a transitory feeling of happiness, and an overall experience of happiness, which does not come from external experiences. Happiness can actually be a distraction. If I want to be happy, I may create activities to promote moments of happiness and things to look forward to. This is what I spent a great deal of my life doing in Vienna, before I met Cees. But what happens when external experiences are no longer enough? What happens when I'm left feeling empty afterward?

Real happiness is something that comes from inside ourselves, and something that can be felt no matter what is happening in our external world. It makes us feel bathed in love and compassion. Real happiness is our natural state—we've simply forgotten it over time.

There's only one way to achieve this happiness: to embrace

all emotions as they arise, without resisting them or wishing they would go away. Paradoxically, even when in the depths of grief, we can feel the sweetness of this permanent happiness. In fact, happiness is found precisely in the hardest emotions to feel. By feeling the pain of losing my mother, I also feel and cherish the love we shared.

Achieving this lasting happiness isn't about something you do—rather, it's about what you *don't* do. First and foremost, you must not avoid emotional tension by using distractions. There are hundreds of things we can do to avoid the discomfort of our emotions. Strangely enough, when we are feeling unease, instead of slowing down to allow for some peace to settle in, we tend to increase activity. It's as if shouting over the voices in our head will drown out the other voices. But by doing that, we only create more noise, which tends to turn into even more confusion.

You'll notice this when your mind jumps from one thought to the next, without any sense of resolution. Quieting this noise in our head goes contrary to our compulsion to move away from pain and unease. Sitting with this unease, in a mode of exploration, is actually the most powerful way to move progressively toward greater happiness.

Imagine that for the last five years you've been unhappy and the tension has moved you to a habit of compulsive eating. Eating becomes a distraction for the unease, and slowly but surely develops into a pattern. Unfortunately, the pattern reinforces itself. The more you eat, the less happy you feel about yourself, and the more you want to eat to pacify the negative emotions. See the pattern forming?

To reverse this, you need resolve. You must say, "No. I do not want this in my life." You add to that the determination of, "Yes, I am going to change." Now you begin the process of losing weight. It doesn't feel good. You often feel irritable and tired. If all you cared about was feeling good in any given moment, you'd quit the process immediately and go back to your old habit. But you know that losing the weight will have benefits that are only felt, for the most part, after the weight has been lost.

With weight, it's easy to see the extra load that we're carrying. With unresolved emotions, it's not quite as visible, but it is just as real. As unresolved pain and suffering enters our lives, it becomes a load, just like excessive weight. We carry it around and it impedes everything we want to achieve. But we continually add to this emotional load and forget how light we felt without it. We forget times when everything felt special and in its place. The emotional burden took over at some point and we lost inspiration and hope.

Removing emotional dead weight is a similar process. And in order to feel better, we will first have to feel much worse. Who would make such a journey? Why would you do something that makes you feel worse, not even knowing if you'll feel better afterwards? This is the paradox. In order to feel the purest happiness, we must first let go of everything that inhibits it from appearing.

The issues that arise are always bigger than people anticipate before taking such a journey. The reason is simple: whatever control or understanding of himself a person thinks he has is confronted in the most dramatic of ways. Think about all the self-identity that is going to be sorted through. I read a study once that suggested a correlation between people in psychiatric wards and higher degrees of consciousness. What this pointed out was that emotional breakdown was a heightened state of awareness that was being diagnosed as mental illness. So instead of embracing the process of release, we have prescribed medication.

I can't tell anyone what will make them happy. However, I can certainly point out how to be unhappy—and that is to hold onto emotional baggage. We do this by resisting pain and suffering. It took me decades to learn the hard way that happiness is what naturally emerges when we learn to embrace all of life—even and especially the hardest parts—without any resistance.

## CHAPTER 39

# ACCEPTANCE AND VULNERABILITY

As children, our natural state is to be curious, courageous, confident, authentic, open, compassionate, and loving. We explore the world without fear or self-doubt. When learning to walk, we get up each time we fall, without criticizing ourselves for falling.

Then we grow older. We start understanding more. What we understand evolves into what we know—or think we know. Thus, we lose much of our natural curiosity. We make more assumptions. We use assumptions to make sense of the things that we do not yet understand. We encounter difficulties when meeting people with other assumptions. We see these people as difficult.

Instead of continually exploring with objective curiosity, we develop a fixed worldview, comprised of assumptions that we never really questioned. Then, everything we experience simply reinforces what we think we already know. We confuse interest with curiosity and we learn more, in the meantime neglecting that there are many things that we understand less.

Over time, we become fearful, closed, judgmental, hardened, and defensive. This happens as we replace our curiosity with perceived "knowledge." But more importantly, it comes as we experience and react to pain. People say and do things that hurt us. We get abused. We experience trauma. We witness death. In these experiences, we desperately try to protect ourselves. Our closed-ness and hard-heartedness are defense mechanisms we use to attempt to avoid pain.

What we fail to realize is that it's precisely by resisting pain that we hold onto pain and make it much worse than it has to be. It's precisely our defense mechanisms that cause the greatest pain. When we let pain be as it is, without resistance, it opens and softens us. It shows us the truth: that we never needed to defend ourselves—the core of our being, the observer within, never needed any protection to begin with. The need for protection was always an illusion.

I have spent most of my life running away from pain. It took me decades to see the joy that was right behind pain. The eighteen-year-old Andy, running to Australia full of pain and sadness, is not all that different than the forty-seven-year-old version sitting in front of his computer today. The difference is that pain has become an old friend. Every sad memory and painful truth leads me back to love and connection, every tear is a beauty to be shared.

I do not profess to know more than anyone else, but I do often find myself more willing to share what's going on in my emotional core. I've spent the past ten years going deep into my old emotional scars until they eventually healed. As I did, it became abundantly clear that life—*every* aspect of it—is beautiful. In allowing myself to be seen, especially in the moments when I feel most inadequate, I feel alive. In having sympathy for my own pain, I feel closer to myself and anyone I'm with at that moment.

I've seen this expression as a bridge for others to embrace the same pain in themselves.

I have found peace with the most painful aspect of life: death. To me, it's a constant reminder of what makes life so wonderful. I have often heard people ask questions like, "What makes life worth living in the face of death? If we all die, why does anything matter? How can we find meaning in life if we all die?"

To me, those are the wrong questions to ask. If we all lived forever, it would be infinitely harder to find meaning in life. Death is precisely what gives life meaning! Death gives us the opportunity to experience the urgency of now.

The inevitability of death is something I hold near and dear. I use it as a guiding light. What would I do differently if I knew I only had a month to live? If I died today, what would I wish I had done?

Writing the letter to my mother. Taking Cees on a trip through the United States. These moments, when I allowed death to create urgency, have defined me. Such thoughts help me find a deeper connection with those around me. If I speak with someone, I never take it for granted that they will be there the next time. It makes for a richer contact, and an intimacy that makes every moment special.

The fundamental keys to a life of meaning and fulfillment, I've learned, are simple: acceptance and vulnerability. We all have our unique sources of anxiety based on our life experiences, be it public speaking, money, health, or relationships. Whatever is rattling around in the back of our heads is not going away. The only way I know how to make peace with fears and anxieties is through the wholehearted acceptance of them.

When we allow ourselves to be vulnerable with our pain, it opens the door to a depth of connection and intimacy with ourselves and others that can be found in no other way. This connection is what makes life worth living. It is the ultimate desire of every human heart.

But sadly, it's what we run away from the most. We're desperately afraid to be ourselves because we worry that we'll be taken advantage of, that people won't see us, that we'll be hurt even more than we have been. Strangely, vulnerability is what we want to see the most in others, but we are often the last ones willing to show it ourselves.

Life is beautiful! All of it, and not just the parts that we put up on our Facebook pages. Allowing for the emotion that follows this truth can be overwhelming. It can be downright scary as hell. But life without that is like eating only dessert without the main course. There is a lot of sugar, but it is not very filling.

If you remember one thing from what I have written, it is this: Be kind to yourself. This life is not easy. There is no guidebook with directions. There are no grades at the end of your stay on this planet. We are all here trying to figure it out. When we see someone who appears to have figured it all out, realize that they too are going home at night and crying. We are often so hard on ourselves that we protect the one thing that gives our lives meaning: vulnerability, letting ourselves be seen as we are.

The things I hear most often in my work are, "I do not feel seen. I do not feel valued. I do not feel loved." Let me assure you that nothing can be further from the truth. The fact that you do not experience love at any given moment does not mean it is not there. I spent twenty years blaming my father for his lack of love, only to realize that I had never been willing to accept him for who he was. So how could I expect him to accept me?

So it is with you. You will find the love and acceptance you seek when you give it to yourself and others. That means accepting yourself, just as you are, in this moment, in all your brokenness, flaws, weaknesses, and pain. It means seeing your cry for love and acceptance in all the ways you act out your pain. And the starting point of the journey is when you open your heart to vulnerability.

## CHAPTER 40

# YOUR LAST LETTER

'd like to invite you to walk through a mental exercise. Imagine this:

> You're sobbing with your head down as you trudge into the mortuary. You see the wooden casket sitting open at the front of the room. It's surrounded by flowers. You shuffle down the aisle, staring at the burgundy carpet.
>
> Your heart breaks for the millionth time, and you break into yet another deep sob as you approach the casket. You pause for a long moment, dredging up courage. Finally, you look inside. You see the body of the person you love more than anyone in the world.
>
> You never had a chance to say goodbye.
>
> Who would this person be for you? And if this were

to happen, what would you wish you had said to him or her, before it was too late?

In Chapter 4, I shared with you the letter I wrote to my mother when I was an eighteen-year-old college student. She read the letter just five hours before she died. Obviously, I had no idea it would be my last letter to her.

That experience drove home to me the fragility of life and the urgency to take meaningful action in the face of mortality. It taught me to take advantage of opportunities to share my love with others. As I've aged, I've learned to do so in open-hearted vulnerability, without hesitation or reservation.

My hope is that my story has inspired you to do the same. We tend to take for granted the people we love the most. We tend to assume they just know how we feel about them, without us needing to tell them all the time. But I ask again: If you knew that you, or someone you loved, would be gone tomorrow, what would that change? What would you say? How would you act differently? How would you treat them differently?

In conclusion, my invitation to you is to write *your* "last letter." Furthermore, I invite you to post a copy of your letter at www.TheLastLetter.com. (You can also read letters there written by other people.) The purpose of the website is to connect all of humanity in love and caring. From one of our greatest shared fears—the fear of loss—we can inspire each other to live more meaningful, joyful lives.

Think of the person whom you love the most. Now, imagine you have one final opportunity to say what he or she means to you. It's your letter, but you may find the following questions helpful as you ponder what you want to say:

- Why are you grateful for this person in your life?
- What particular things has this person done for you that you find meaningful or special?

- If this person were to die, what would you miss the most about him or her?
- What are your favorite memories with this person?
- What have you always wanted to say to this person but have felt incapable of saying, or perhaps just couldn't find the words?
- If you didn't have a chance to say goodbye to this person, what would you regret not being able to say to him or her?

Seriously considering the reality that this person will eventually be gone—and could be gone any moment—may be more painful for you than you want to deal with. But as I've learned, it's precisely by facing the pain of this reality that we find meaning in life. Pain is the price we pay for love. If we didn't care about anyone, we wouldn't be hurt by their loss. But the pain of loss is evidence of our love. Acting from that pain is how we find connection and meaning.

In 1997, a college class changed my life forever. I imagined my suffering, and I took that opportunity to write the last message I would ever send to my mother. I now invite you to take the same opportunity. Meaning is now at your fingertips.

Please don't let the moment pass—because you don't know if you'll ever have another chance.

Love,
Andy

–

**P.S.**

If you find this letter writing exercise meaningful, then I have a challenge for you to take it to the next level.

Think of the person you've struggled with the most in your life, someone who has been to you what my father was to me—perhaps a parent, a sibling, or an estranged friend, anyone who has hurt you deeply, or the person you'd be most frightened to send a letter of love and compassion to.

In your relationship with this person, ask yourself:

- Where am I in avoidance?
- Where have I been afraid that I would be judged?
- How have I judged this person?
- In what ways have I not truly seen, understood, and accepted this person?
- Where have I given up?
- What do I need to let go of?

Imagine that person in your mind and, instead of observing them with judgment, frustration or anger, see them as the imperfect, incapable person that they are. Now imagine yourself writing to them and telling them how special they are and how incapable you were of seeing the parts of them that were not always easy to be with.

Now, your challenge is to write a "last letter" to this person. Do you accept? Can you find it in yourself to see this person and reach out in love and compassion? If so, I would love to read your letter. Please feel free to share it at www.TheLastLetter.com.

# CHAPTER PHOTO INDEX

Welcome: Camden Markets (Camden Town, England 2018)

Chapter 1: Church (Barcelona, Spain 2017)

Chapter 2: Biennale art installation (Venice, Italy 2017)

Chapter 3: The Plague Column (Vienna, Austria 2017)

Chapter 4: Book on stairs (Amsterdam, The Netherlands 2018)

Chapter 5: Omaha Beach Cemetery (Normandy, France 2017)

Chapter 6: Park (Bucharest, Romania 2015)

Chapter 7: Desert (Las Vegas, USA 2009)

Chapter 8: Pablo Neruda House (Isle Negra, Chile 2015)

Chapter 9: John Pence Art Gallery (San Francisco, California 2016)

Chapter 10: Rani climbing Steinernen Meer (Salzburg, Austria 2017)

Chapter 11: Bathroom sign (Kyoto, Japan 2014)

Chapter 12: Mont Saint-Michel (Brittany, France 2017)

Chapter 13: Festival float (Shinjo, Japan 2014)

Chapter 14: Two girls (Tokyo, Japan 2014)

Chapter 15: Outdoor market (Udaipur, India 2013)

Chapter 16: Graffiti (Valparaiso, Chile 2015)

Chapter 17: Winery (Mendoza, Argentina 2015)

Chapter 18: Mountain Range (Chamonix, France 2017)

Chapter 19: Crocodile farm (West Java, Indonesia 2014)

Chapter 20: Climbers (Mount Blanc, France 2017)

Chapter 21: Home of Jules Verne (Amiens, France 2017)

Chapter 22: Paint cans at Musical Arts Center (Bloomington, USA 2018)

Chapter 23: Hood ornament (Sebastopol, California 2014)

Chapter 24: Mirror maker (Venice, Italy 2017)

Chapter 25: Shop on Kartnerstrasse (Vienna, Austria 2017)

Chapter 26: Bryce Canyon (Southwestern Utah, USA 2014)

Chapter 27: Stairs (Valparaiso, Chile 2015)

Chapter 28: Church (Guerande, France 2017)

Chapter 29: Kids hanging on fence (Budapest, Hungary 2017)

Chapter 30: Signs wearing away (Barcelona, Spain 2017)

Chapter 31: Amiens Cathedral (Amiens, France 2017)

Chapter 32: Child on shoulders (San Sebastian, Spain 2017)

Chapter 33: Cemetery (Murano, Italy 2017)

Chapter 34: Science museum (London, England 2018)

Chapter 35: Biennale art installation (Venice, Italy 2017)

Chapter 36: Oxford Street (London, England 2018)

Chapter 37: Wooden bridge to the ocean (Sardina, Italy 2013)

Chapter 38: Clouds (location and date unknown)

Chapter 39: Jules Verne Statue (Amiens, France 2017)

Chapter 40: Shop window Prinsengracht (Amsterdam, The Netherlands 2018)

CPSIA information can be obtained
at www.ICGtesting.com
Printed in the USA
LVHW090201120920
665713LV00003B/496